# Chandler Klebs Black and White Art

This book contains most of my designs from previous books but only the black and white pictures. No other colors than these two are allowed in this book! This means it prints at a cheaper cost to me which means a lower price for those who buy it! I am also not allowing shades of gray because the purpose is two show what the world would look like in black and white which is of course impossible in the real world. People say that I only see things in black and white. After seeing this book, they will know they are right!

I have been doing art in Inkscape for years and have lost much of the originals. There are over 1000 drawings published on the internet. One of my greatest fears has been the site going extinct and all my art being deleted. Because of this I began a project of collecting what I consider to be the best of my art and collecting the SVG files and/or recreating them. This way I won't lose them. It also means people can look at this book to see my art. Not everyone at this current time knows how to use computers and yet they may still like my art. I'm hoping to make a serious business out of designing art for people the way they like. The pictures in this book serve as examples of what I can do.

Almost all of these were designed using the open source software: Inkscape. It's probably the greatest program of all time for doing my style of 2D polygon art.

You can view my art in the places I've published it. The best place is my deviantart gallery where pretty much everything I've ever done exists.

https://10binary.deviantart.com/gallery/

I've also uploaded tons of stuff to Society6 so it is available for sale to be printed on a variety of products.

https://society6.com/chandlerklebs

If you find something you really like, please tell me and I can make it available in the size and colors you like!

email:
chandlerklebs@gmail.com

Most of the pages of this book are all pictures! At the top of each page I did my best to include the title based on the file names as I imported them. This is the same process I did when I uploaded them to society 6 and therefore will help people find them on there if they search for that same name.

Also, an interesting fact you may want to know is that I really love horses. It is for that reason that my pictured "Chessboard Unicorn" was made. Unicorns are simply horses that have a horn on their forehead and commonly produce rainbows. The reason that I like horses so much has to do with their peaceful personality and the fact that they, like other herbivores, eat only plants. I'm an ethical vegan and it's important to mention that I will not make art that in any way advertises or promotes the use of animal products since obtaining meat, dairy, eggs, and honey because most, if not all of the time requires humans to continually breed and kill animals as standard industry practice. Same goes for leather, fur, or other uses of animals that either cause pain to or require killing for the selfish desires of humans who have other options for what they eat, wear, or entertain themselves with.

# Puzzle Trigon

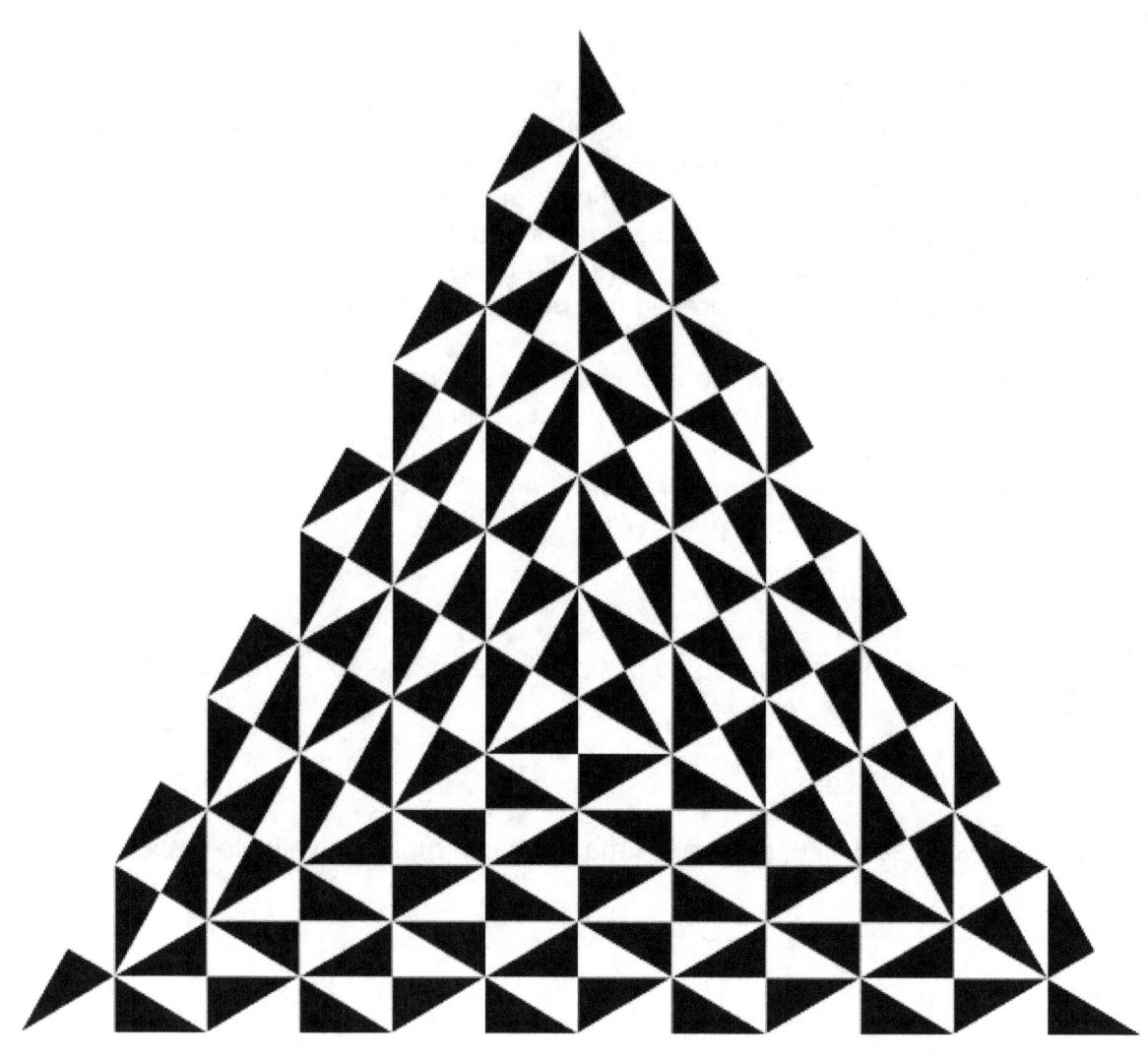

# 6 Chessboard Rainbow Hexagon

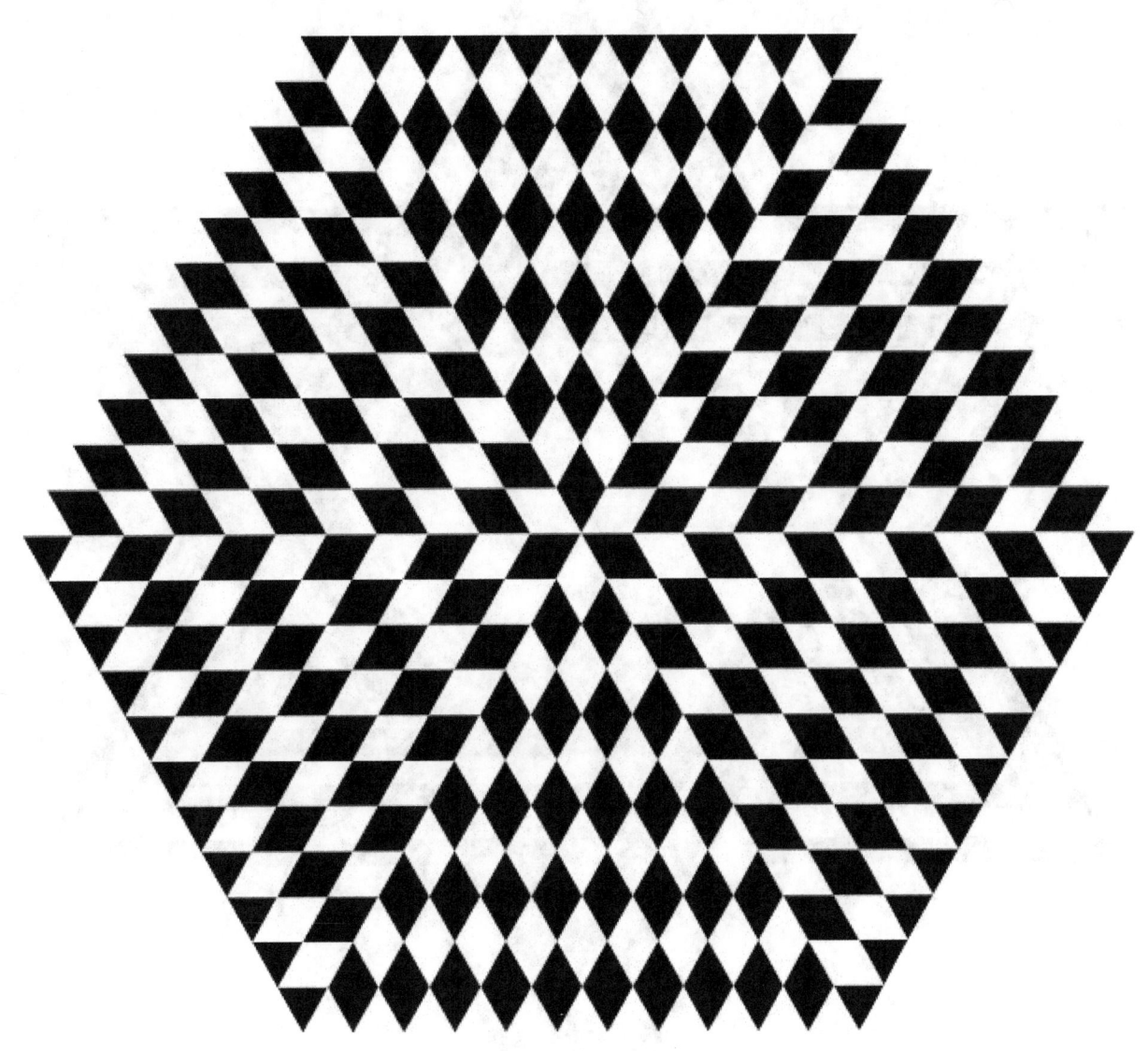

# Six Stripe Hexagram Black and White

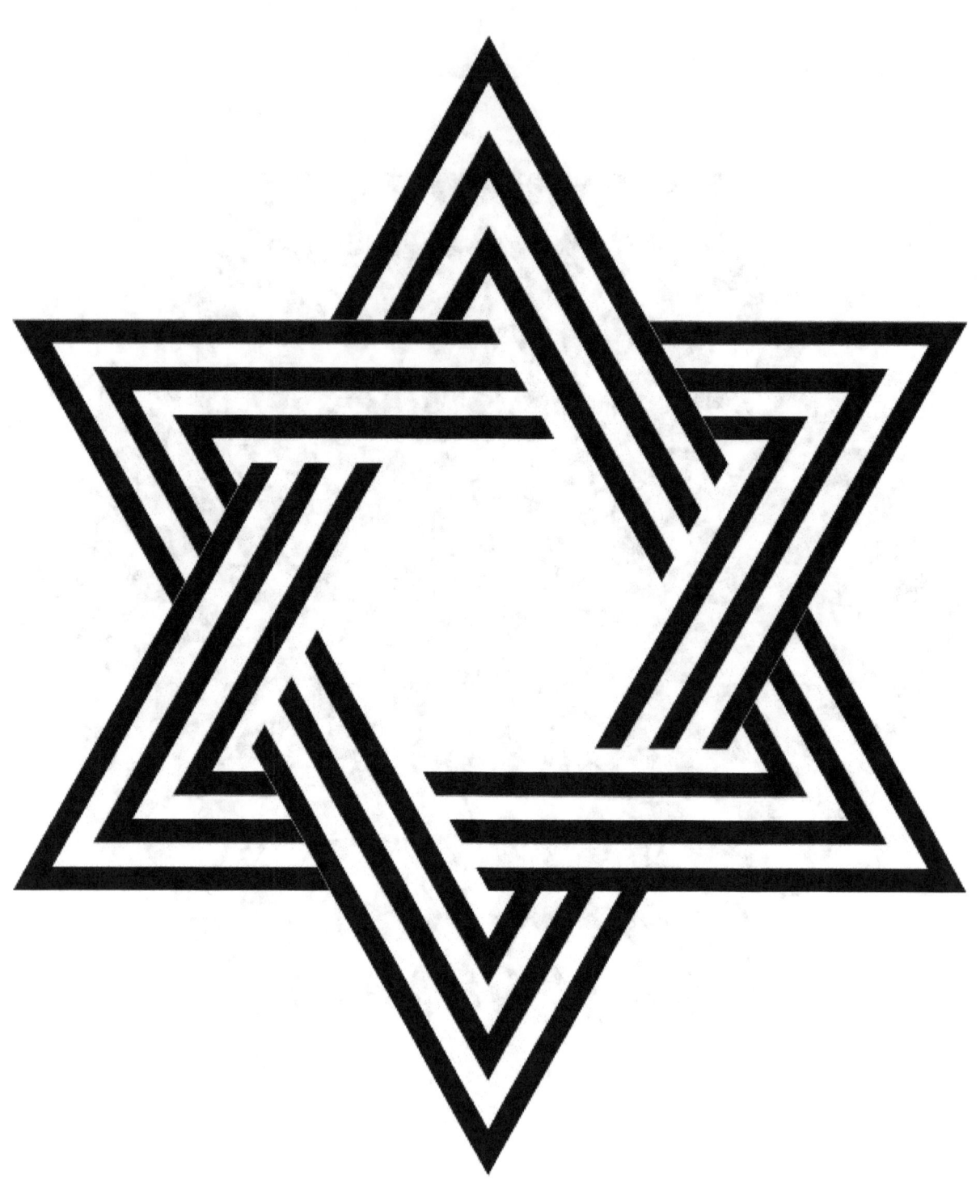

# Very Strange Pentagram

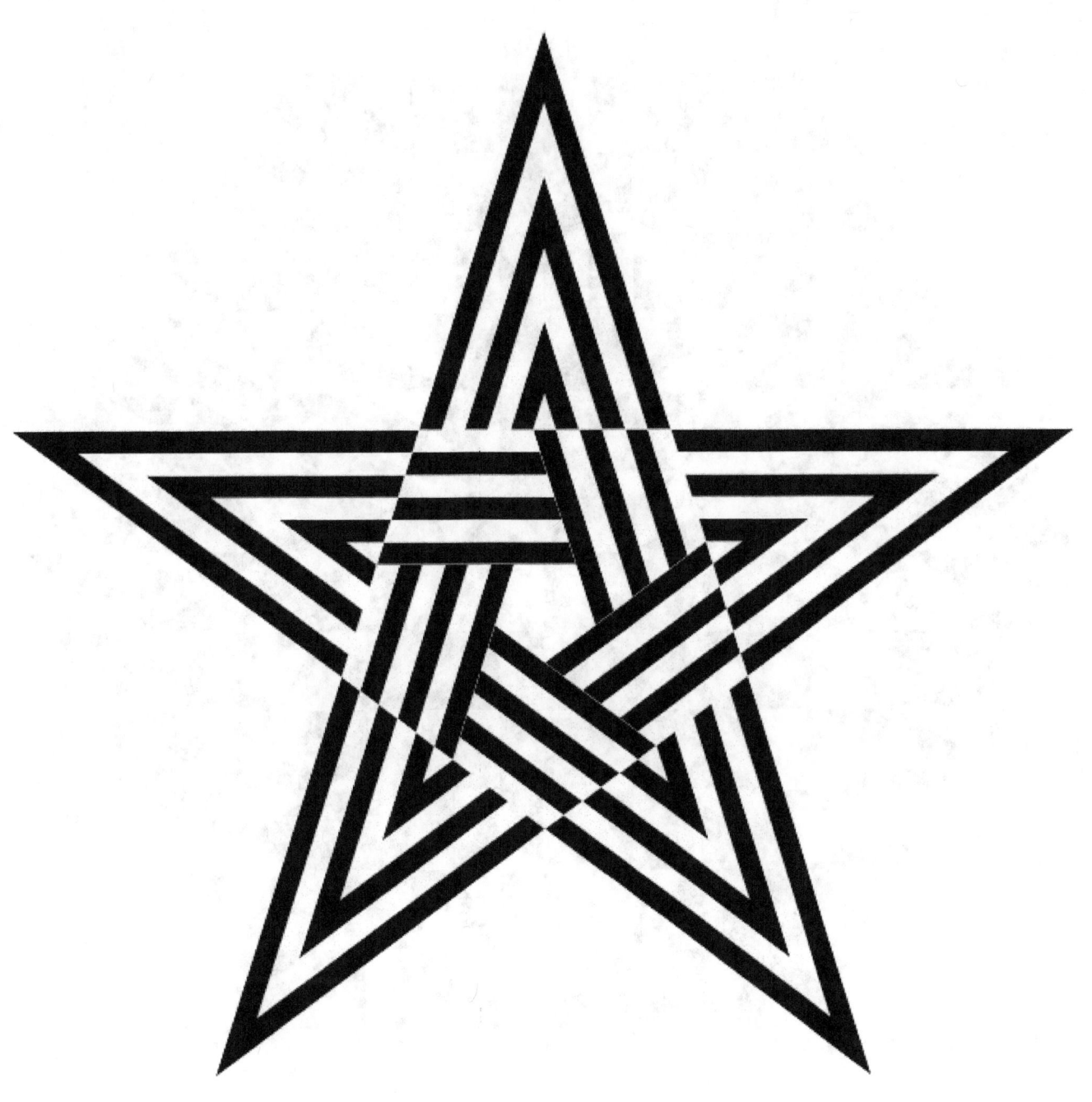

# Puzzle Hexagon

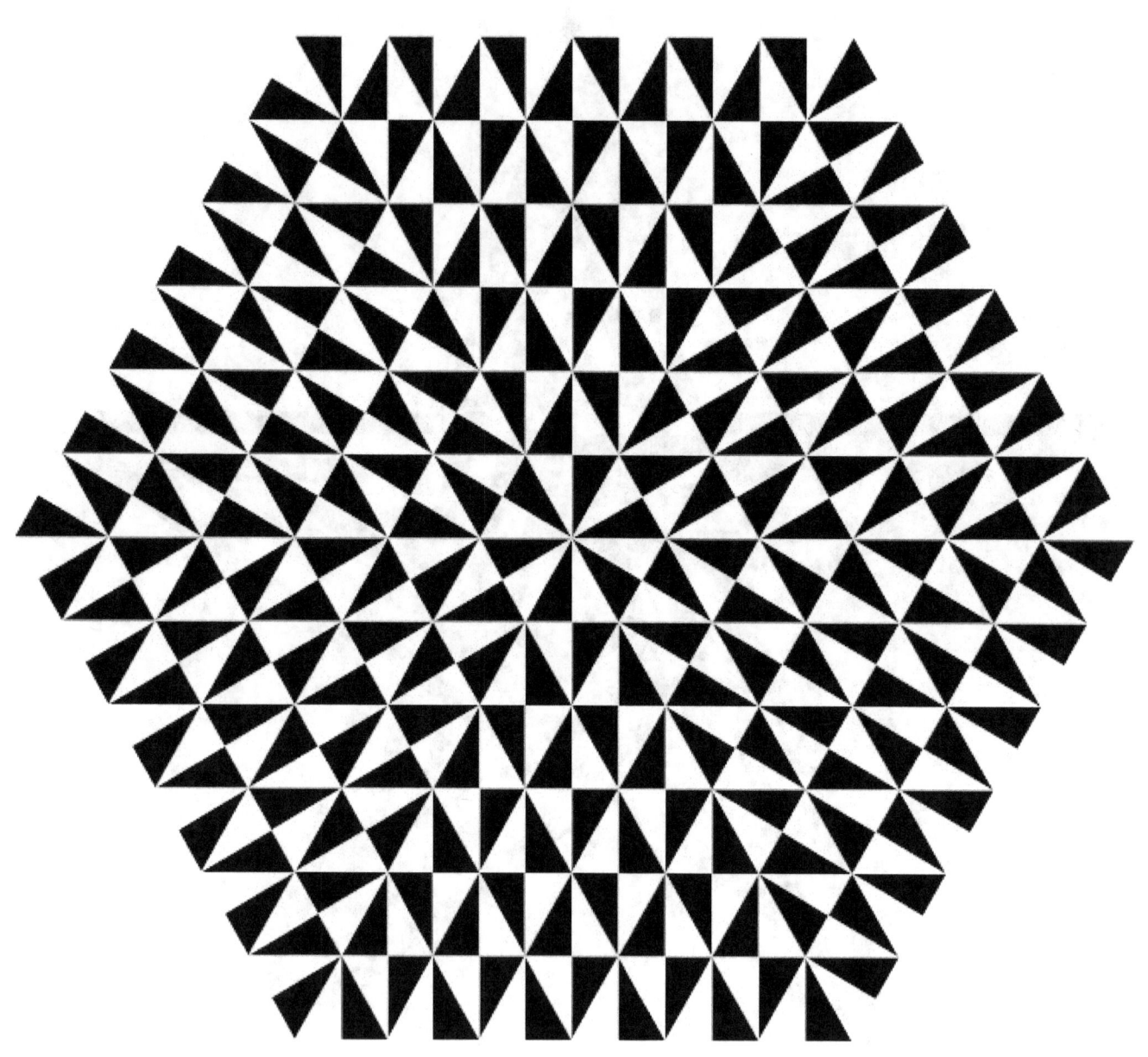

# Puzzle Pentagon

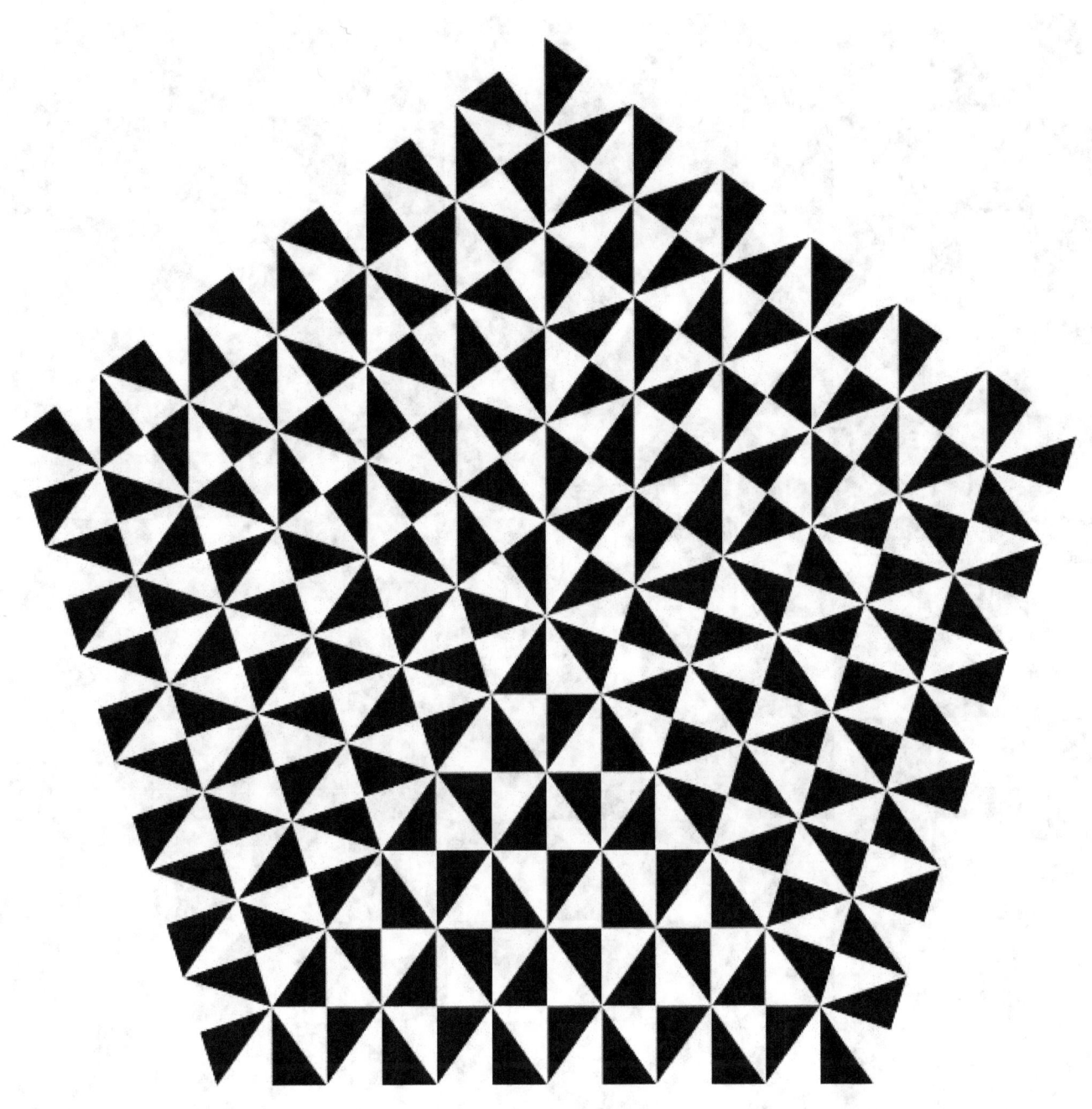

# Puzzle Square

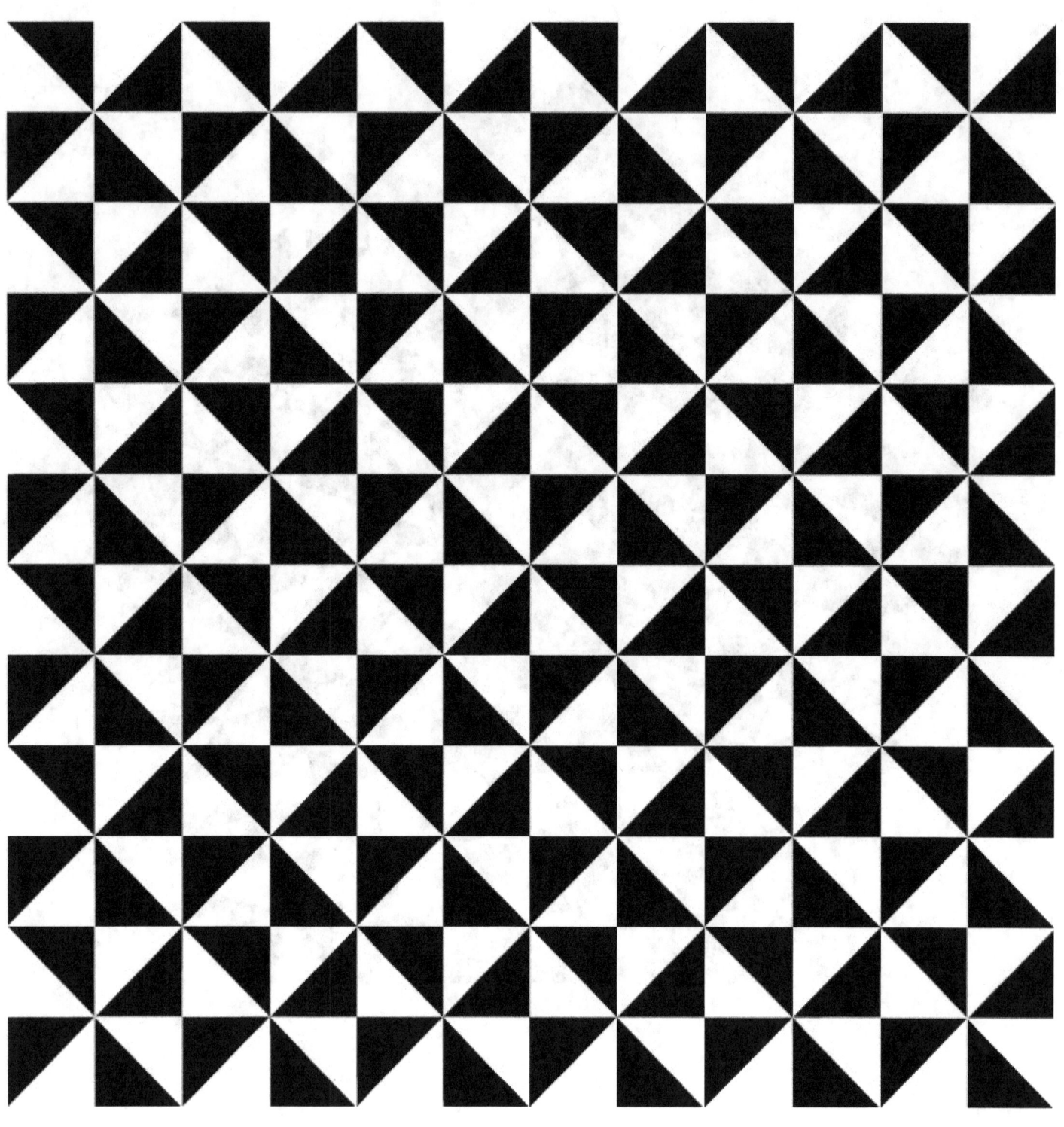

# Chessboard Unicorn

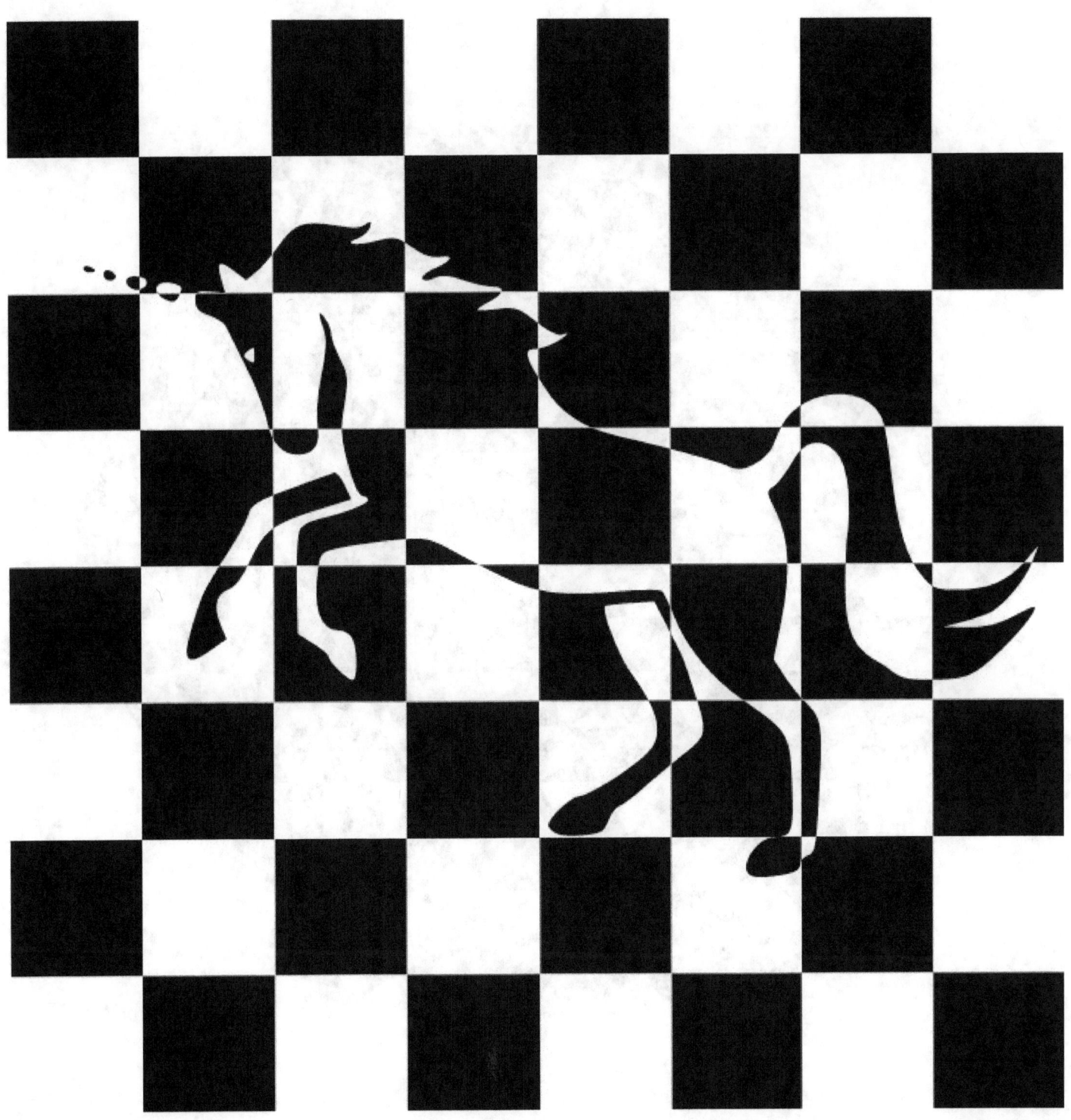

# Hexagon of Black and White Triangles

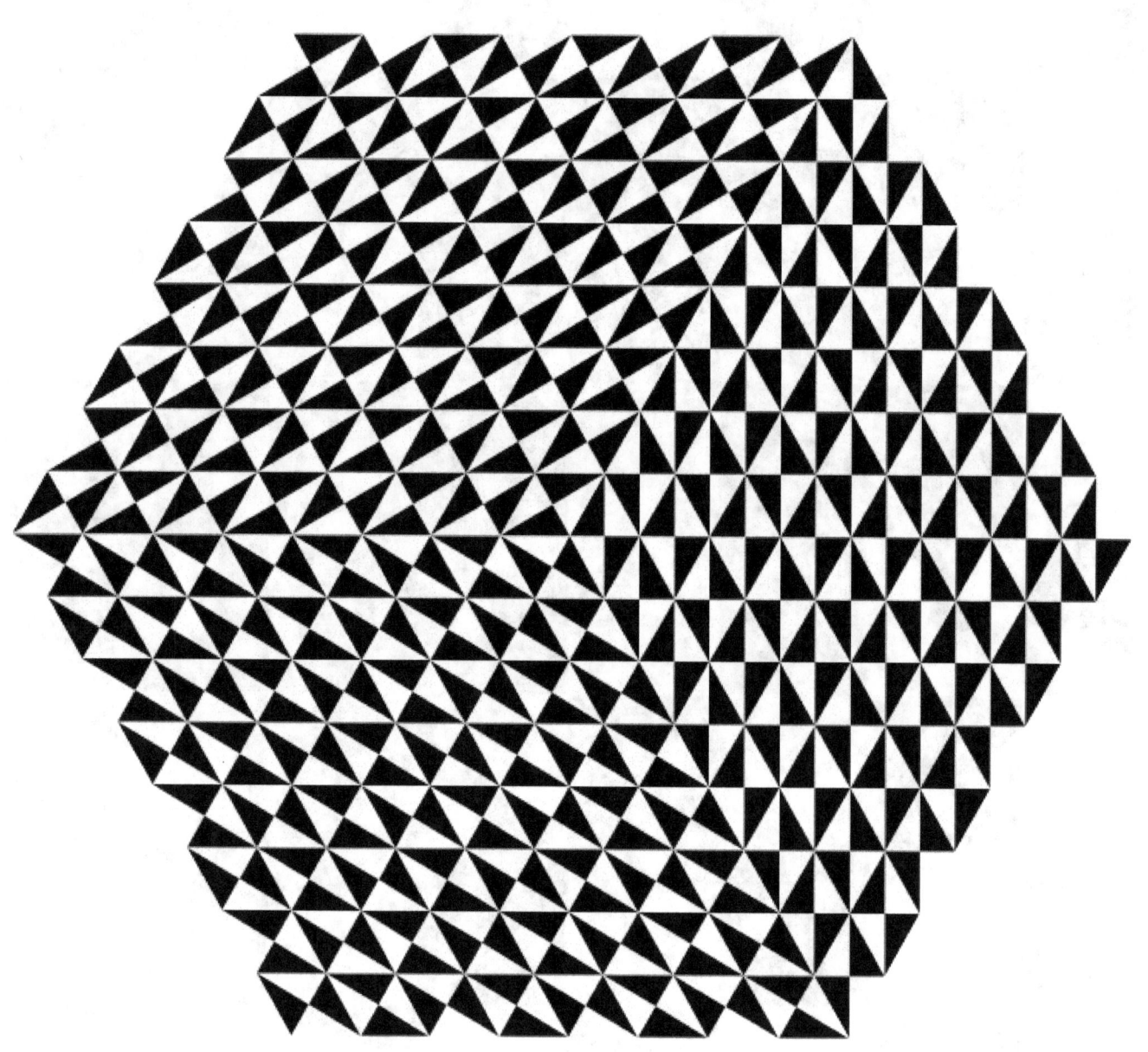

# Chessboard 24x24

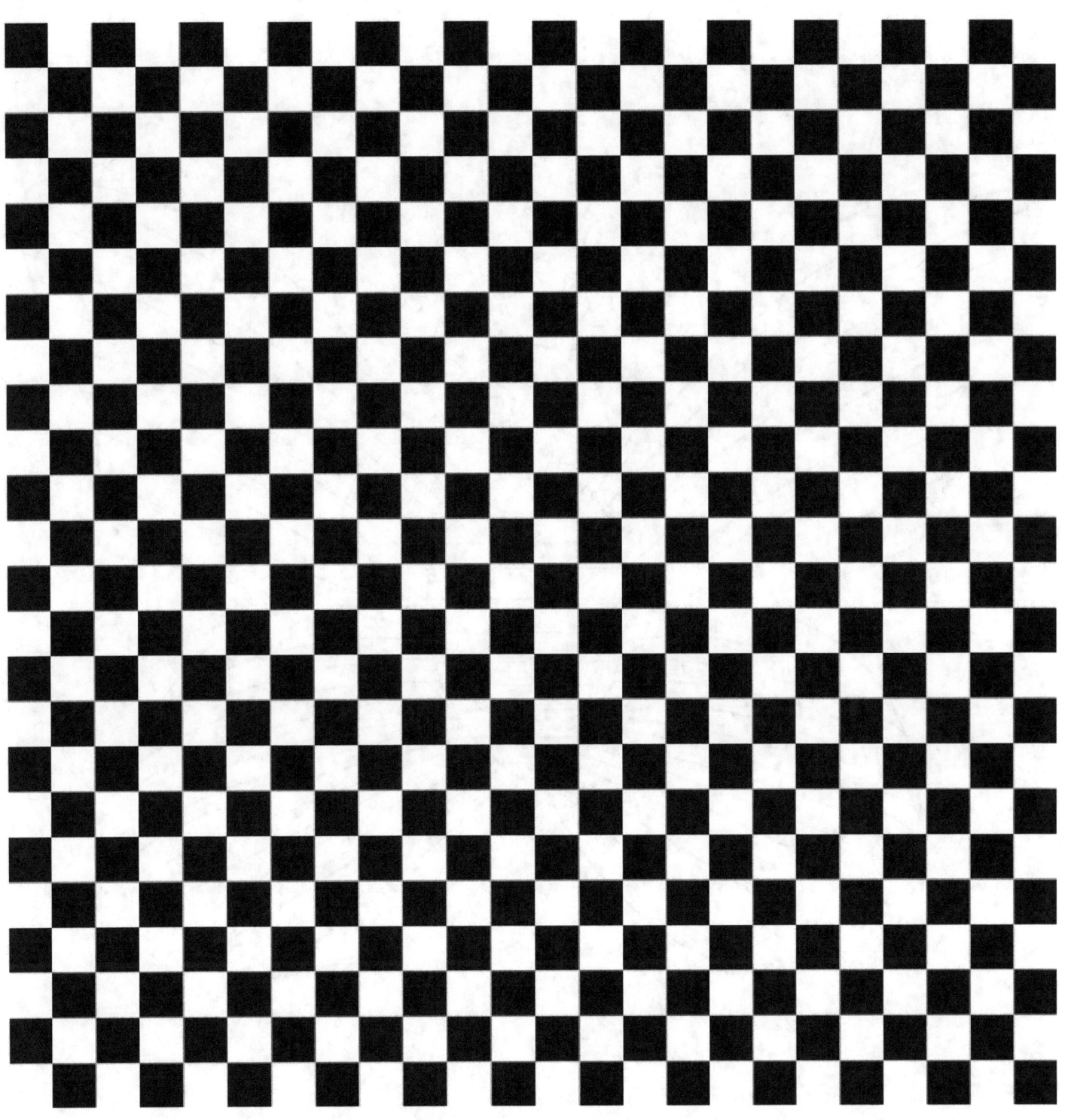

# Butterfly

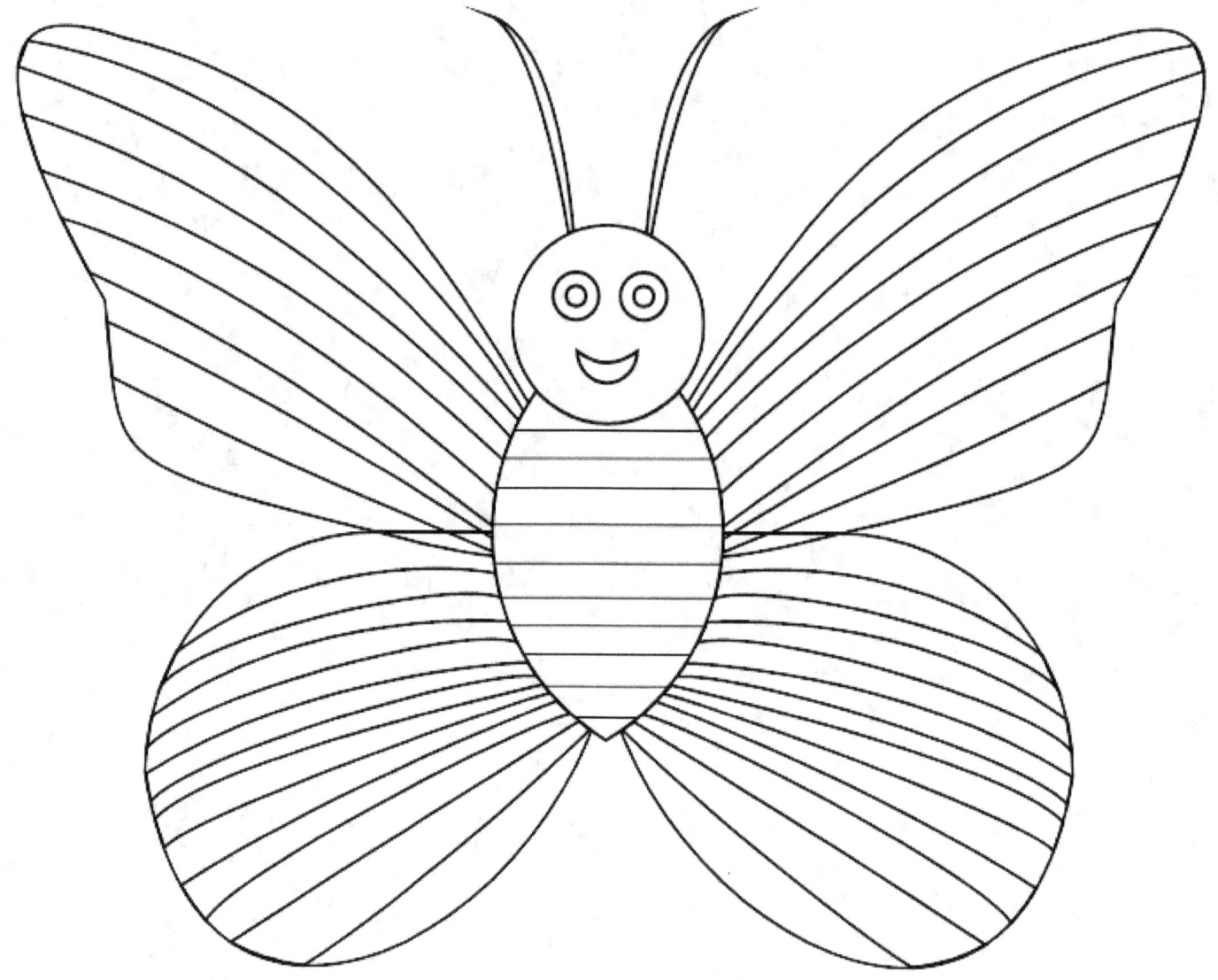

# Triangle Tessellation

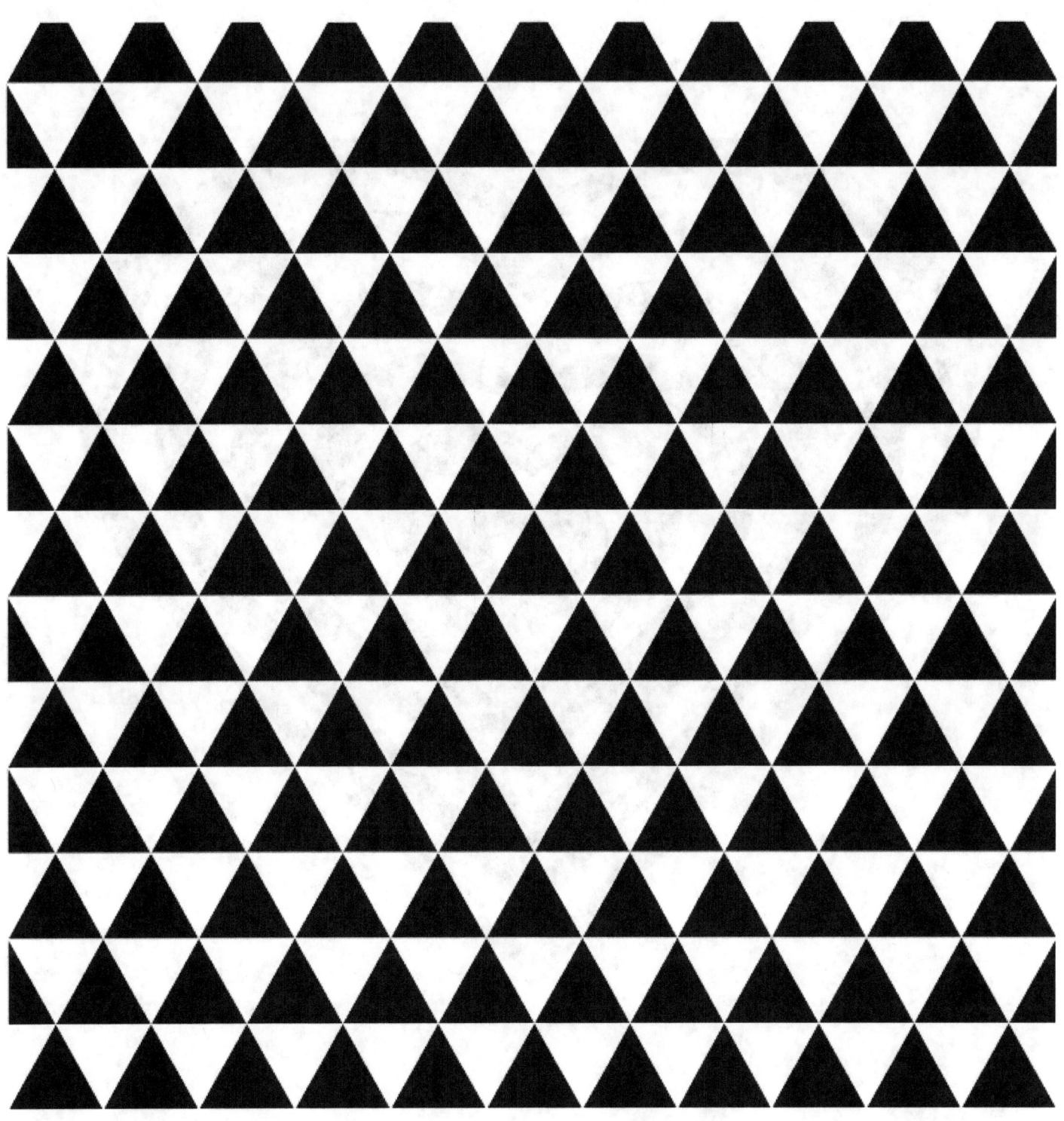

# Zebra Heart

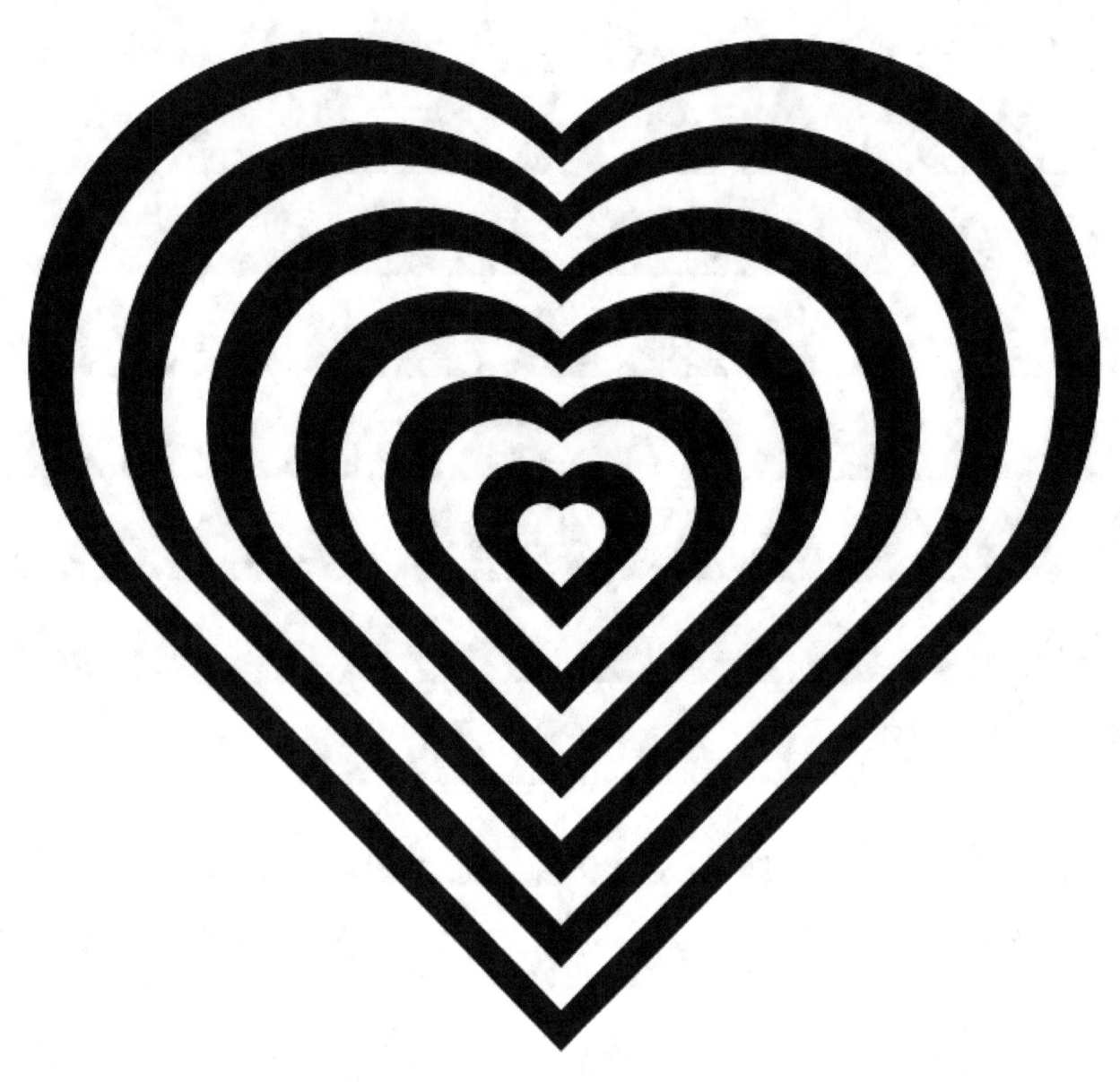

# The Eye of Eternity

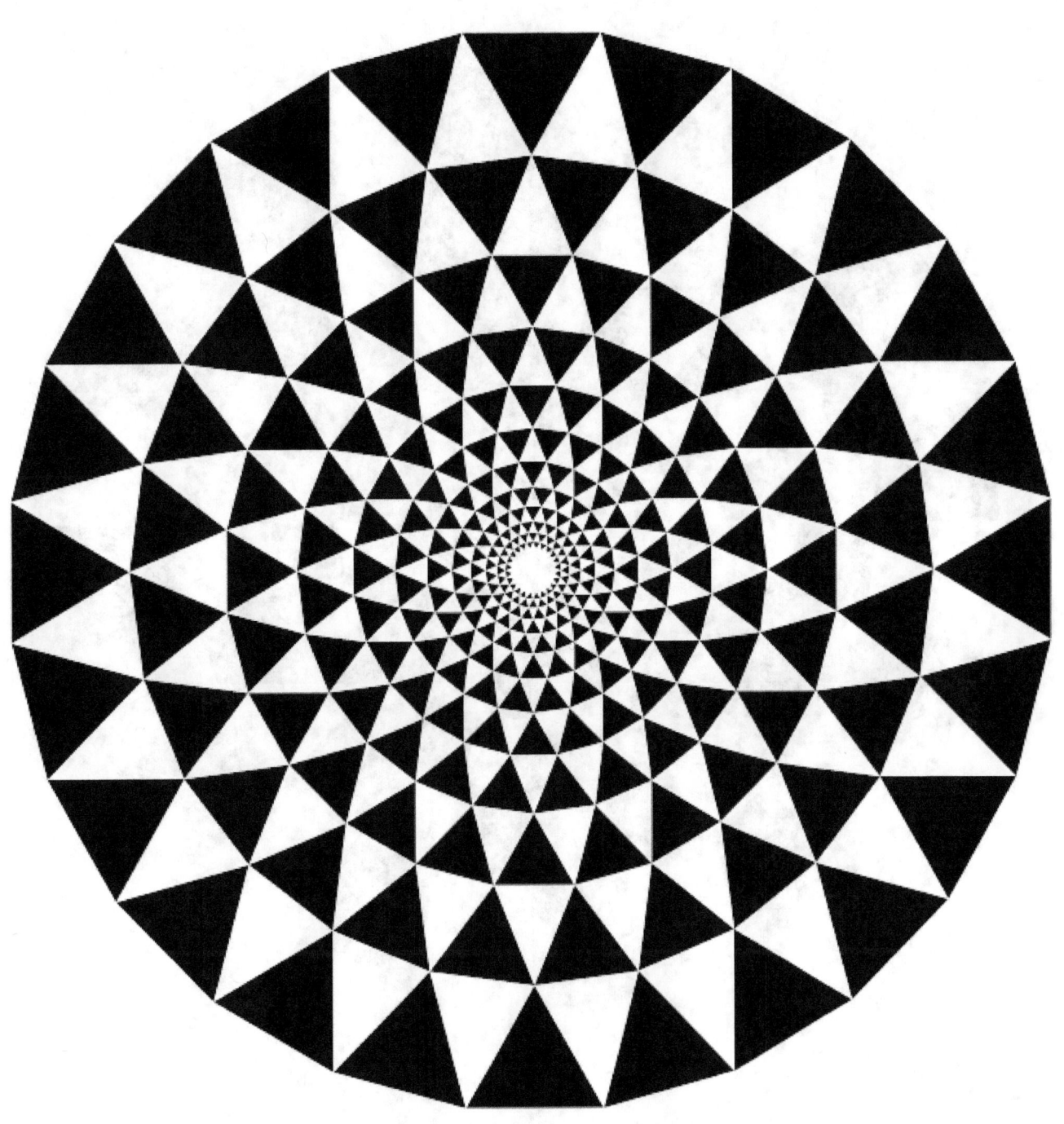

# Checker Tunnel

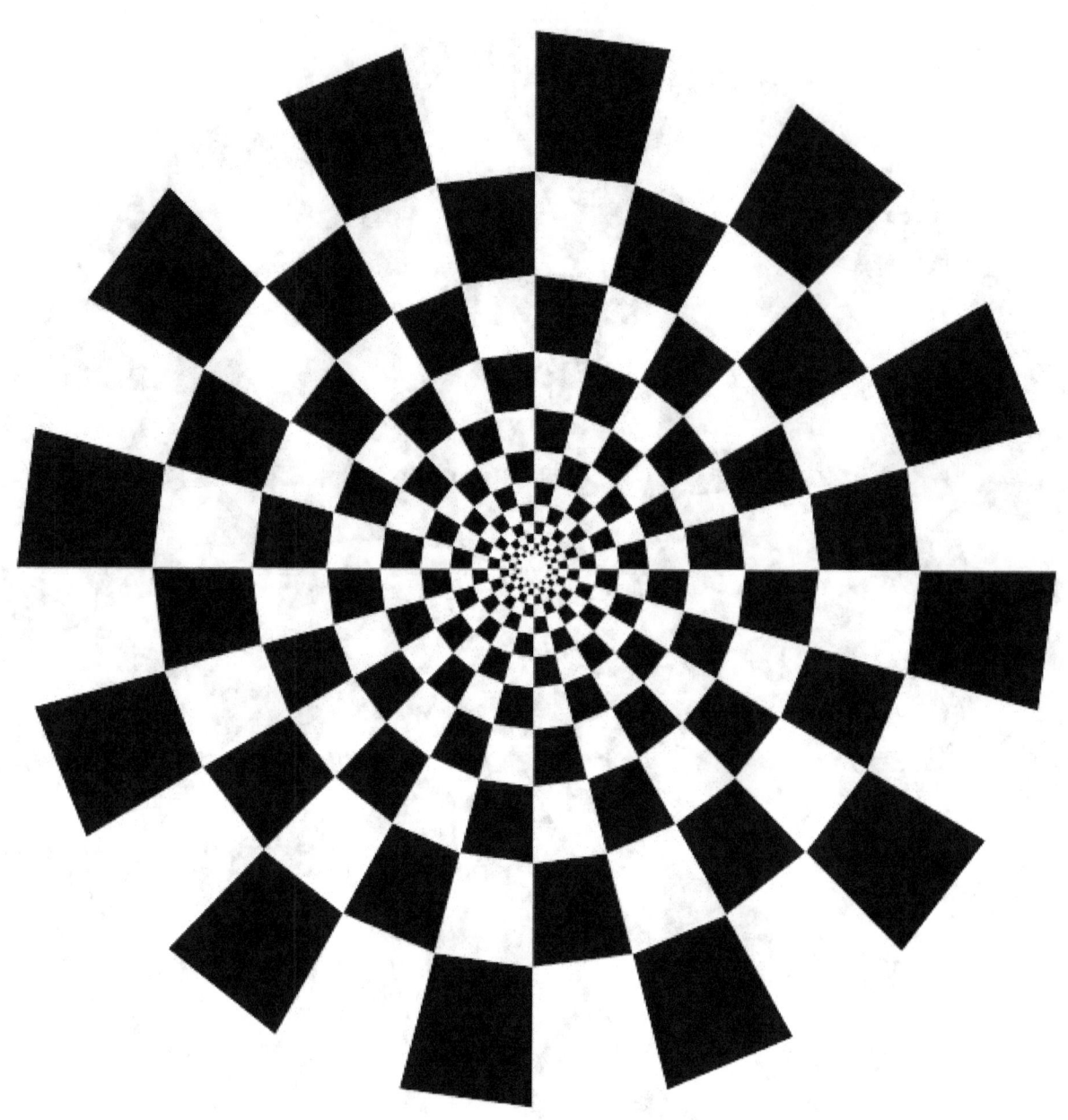

# Checkerplanet 60gon

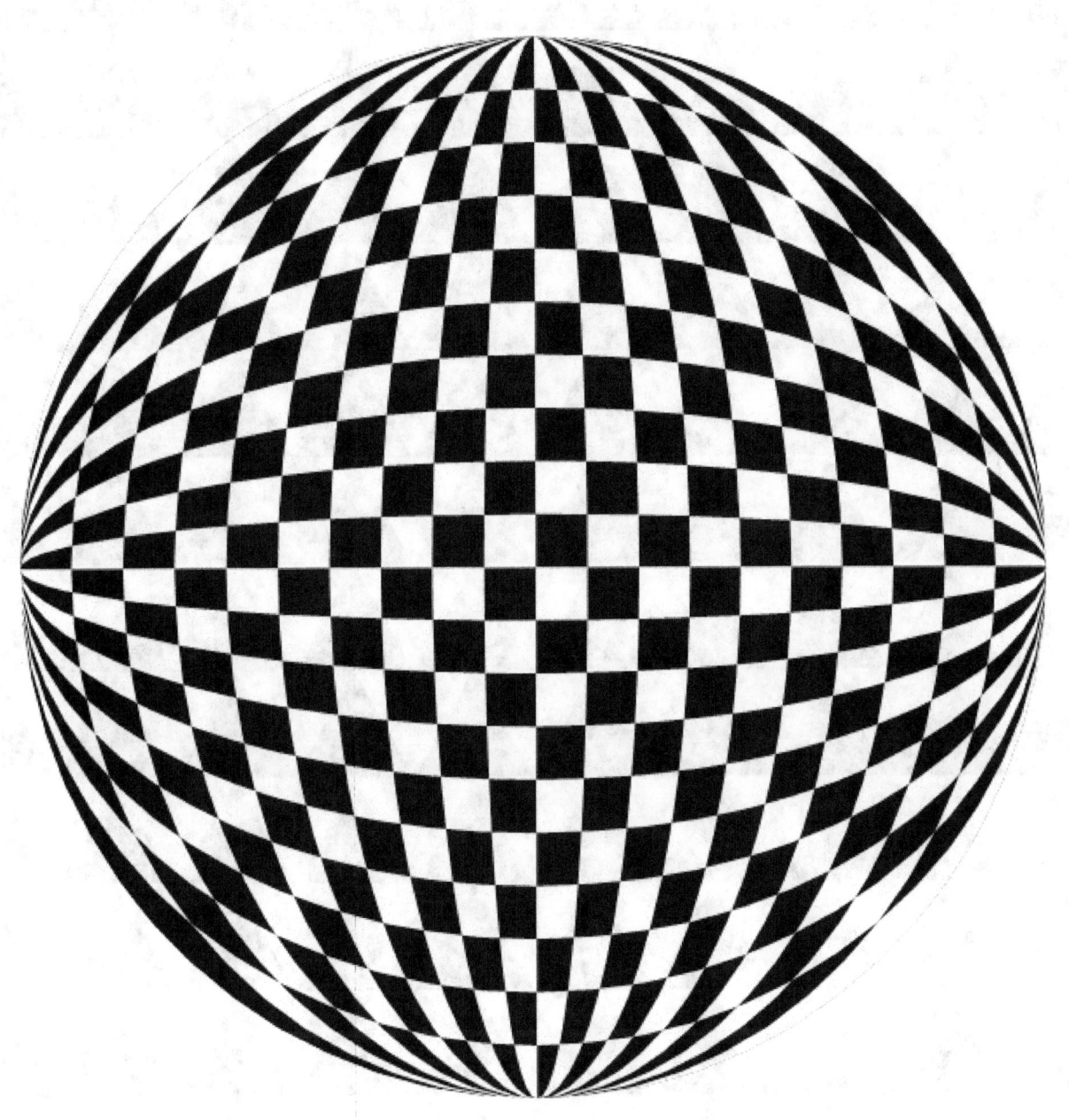

# Triangles Up and Down

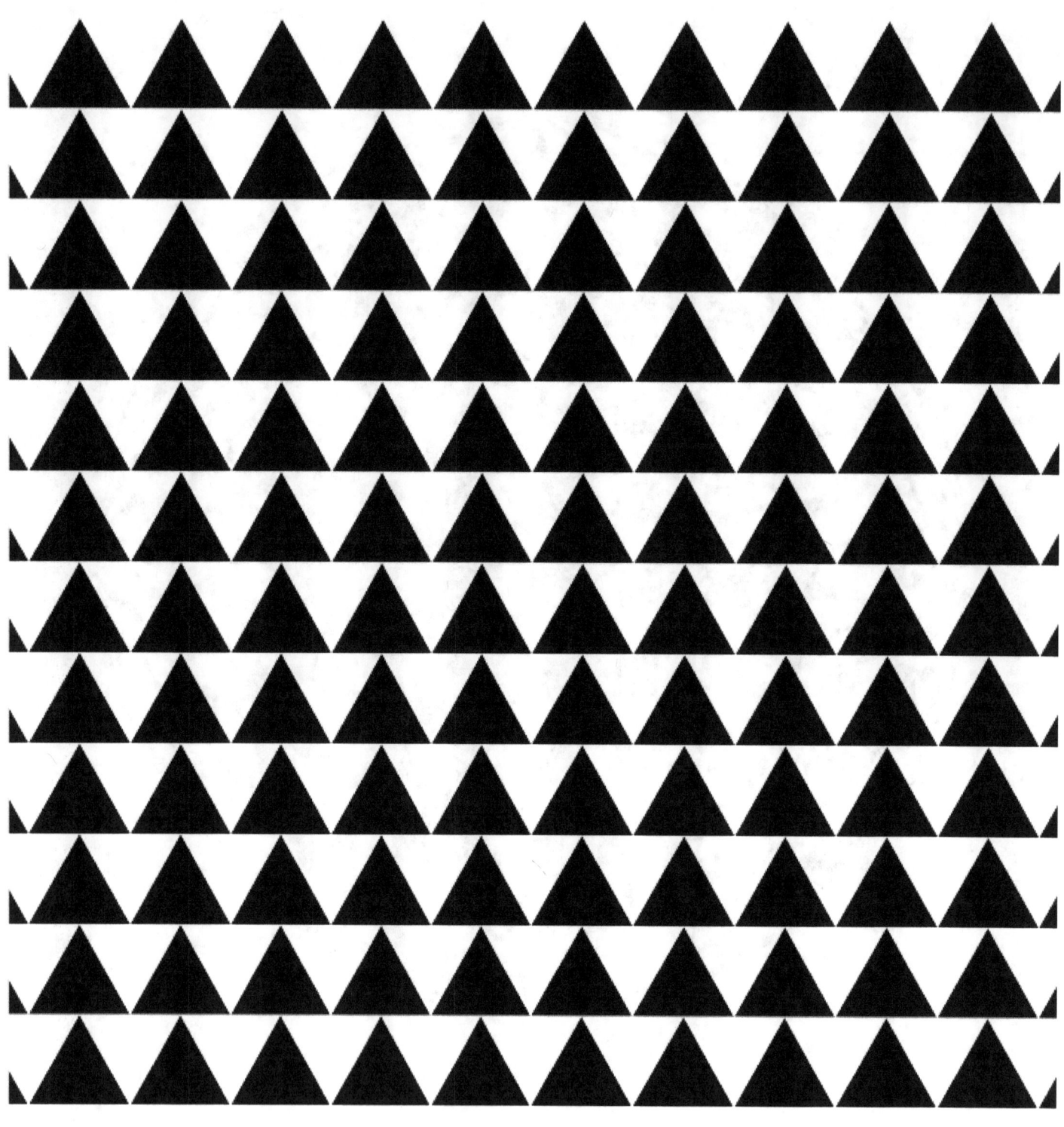

# Triangalight Excite

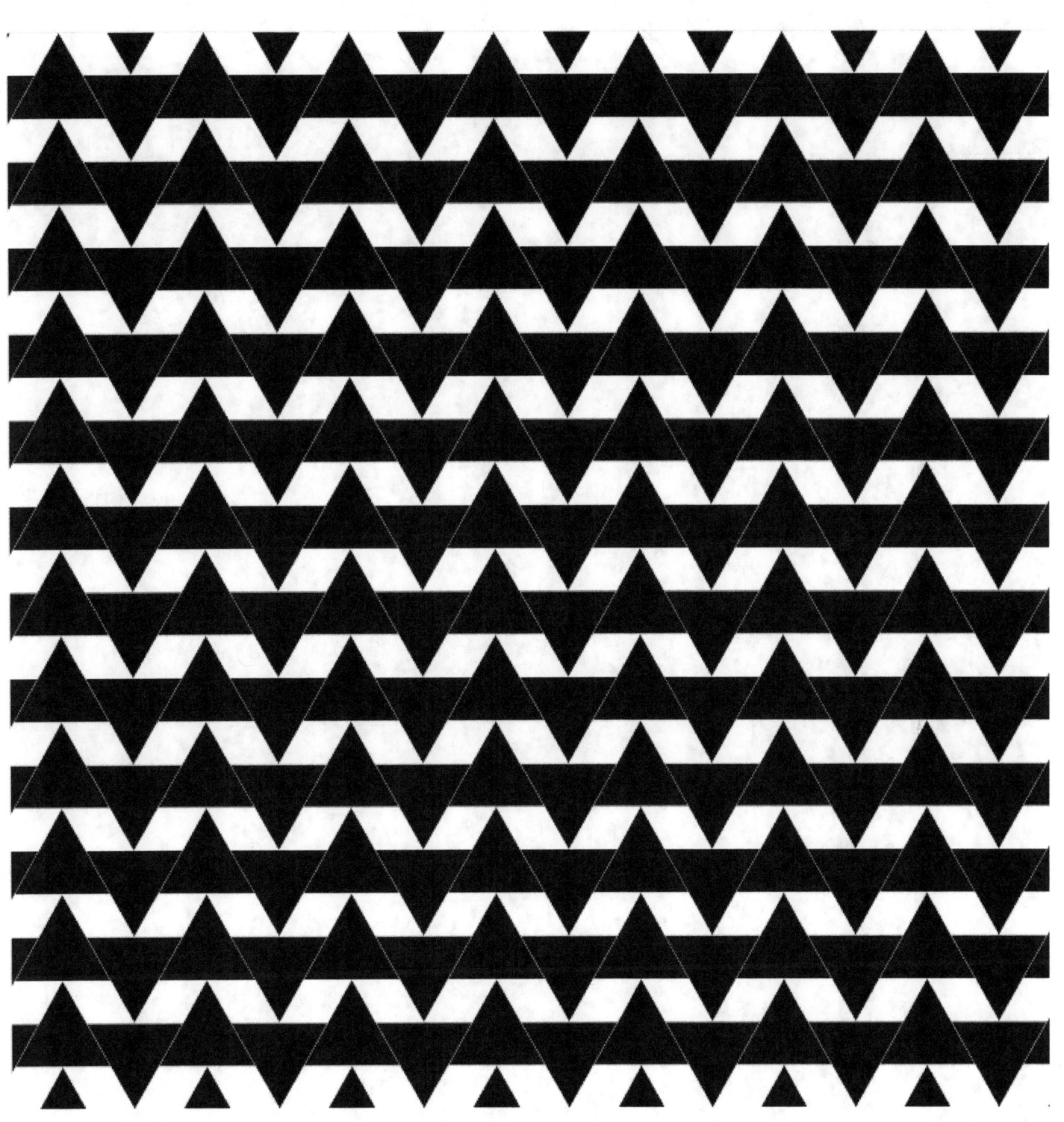

# Bunny

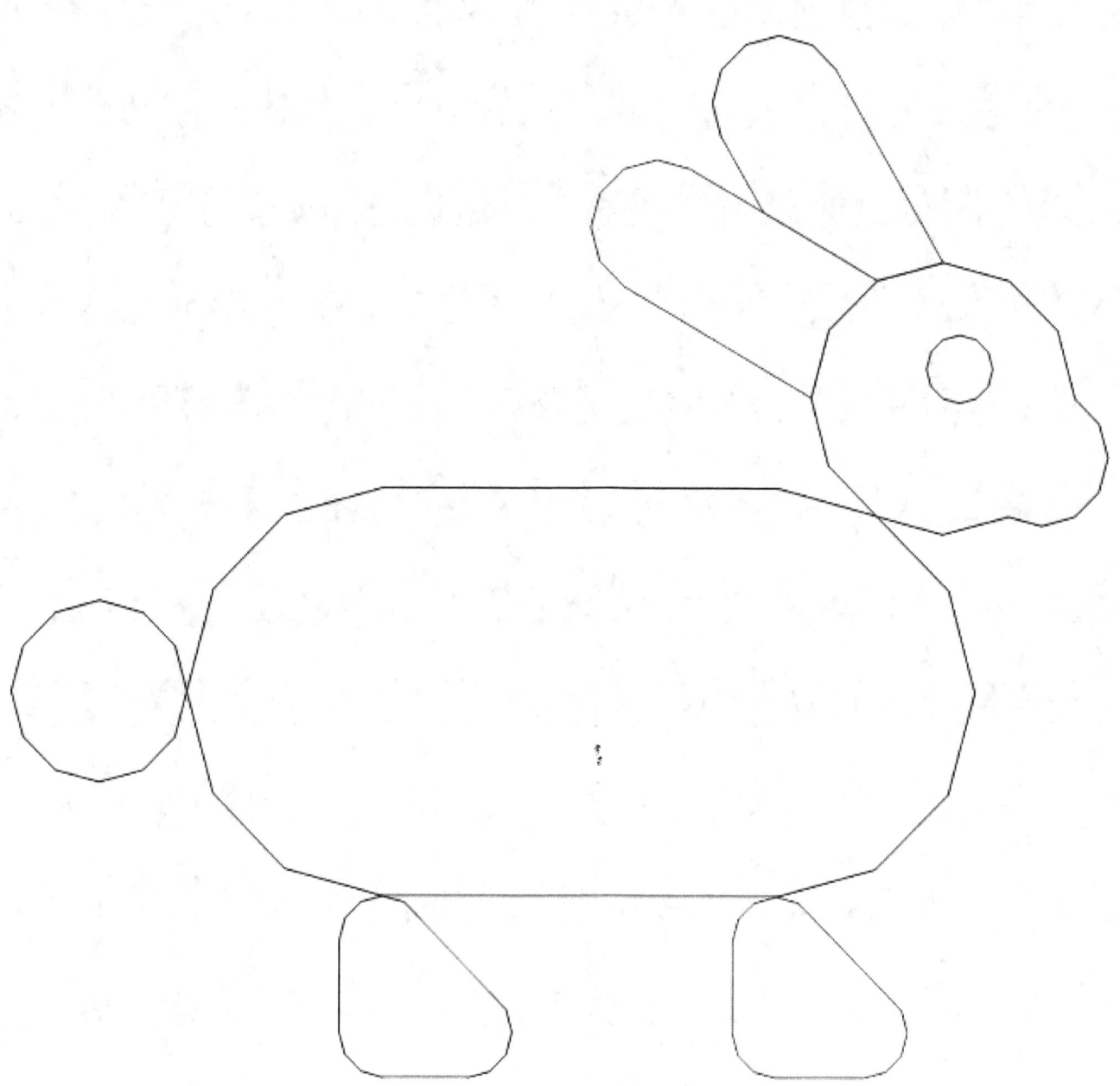

# 19-9-Star-white on black

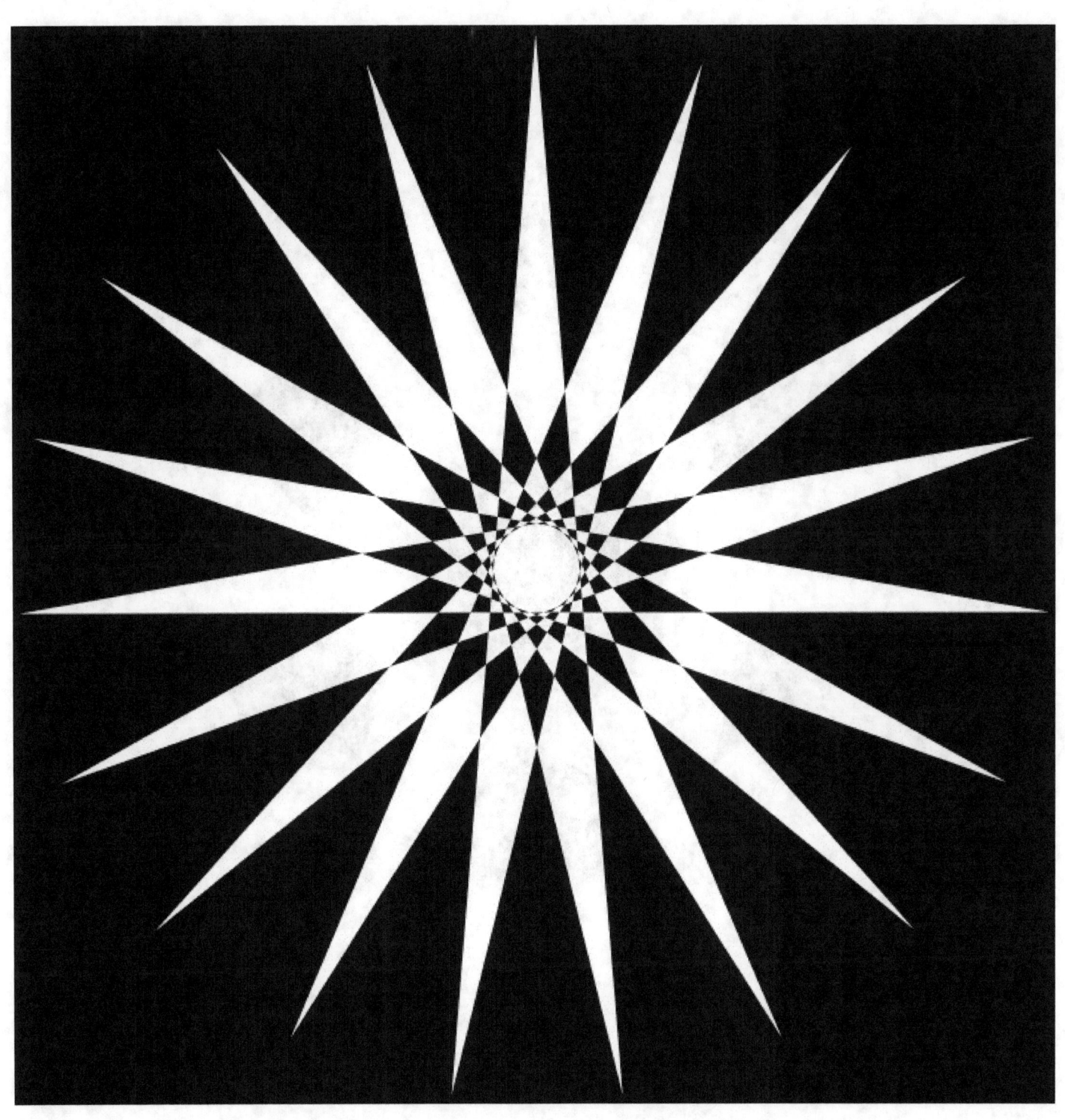

# Seven Deadly Shapes Black

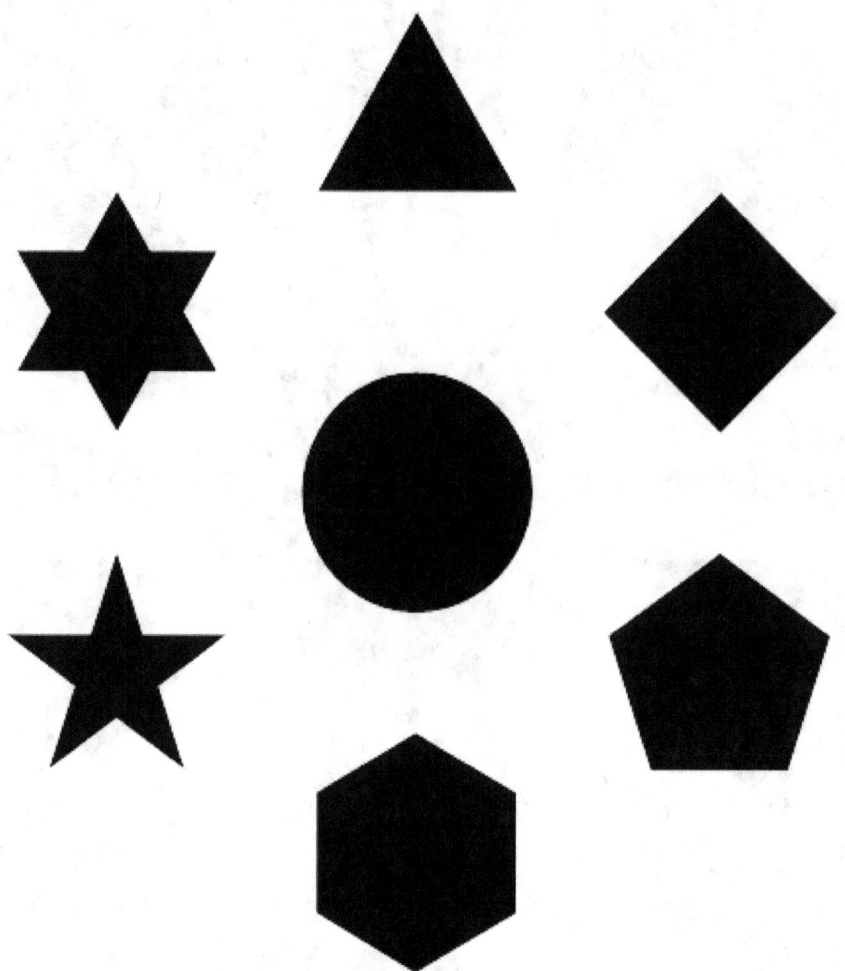

# Metatron's Cube

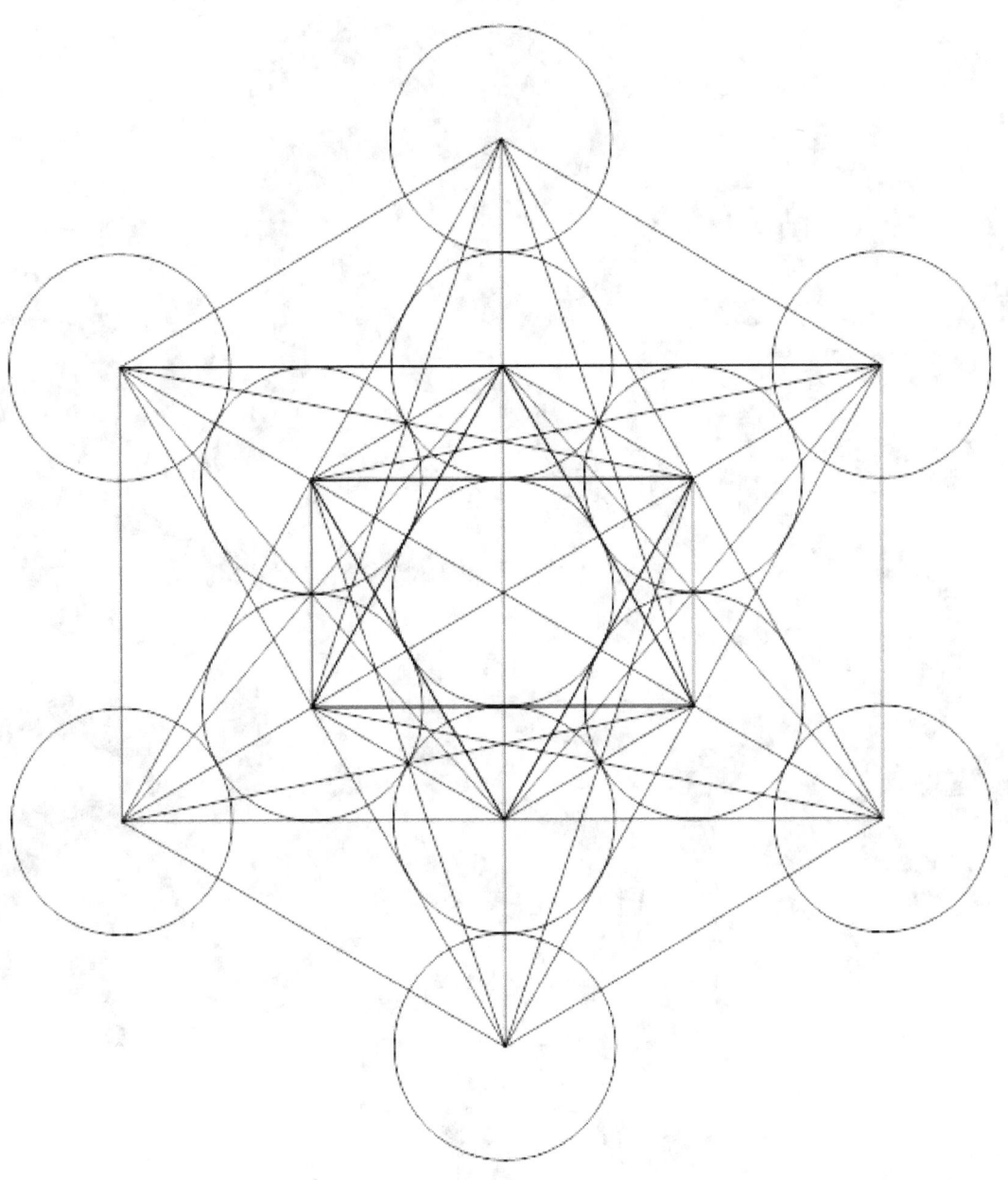

# Zebra Chaos

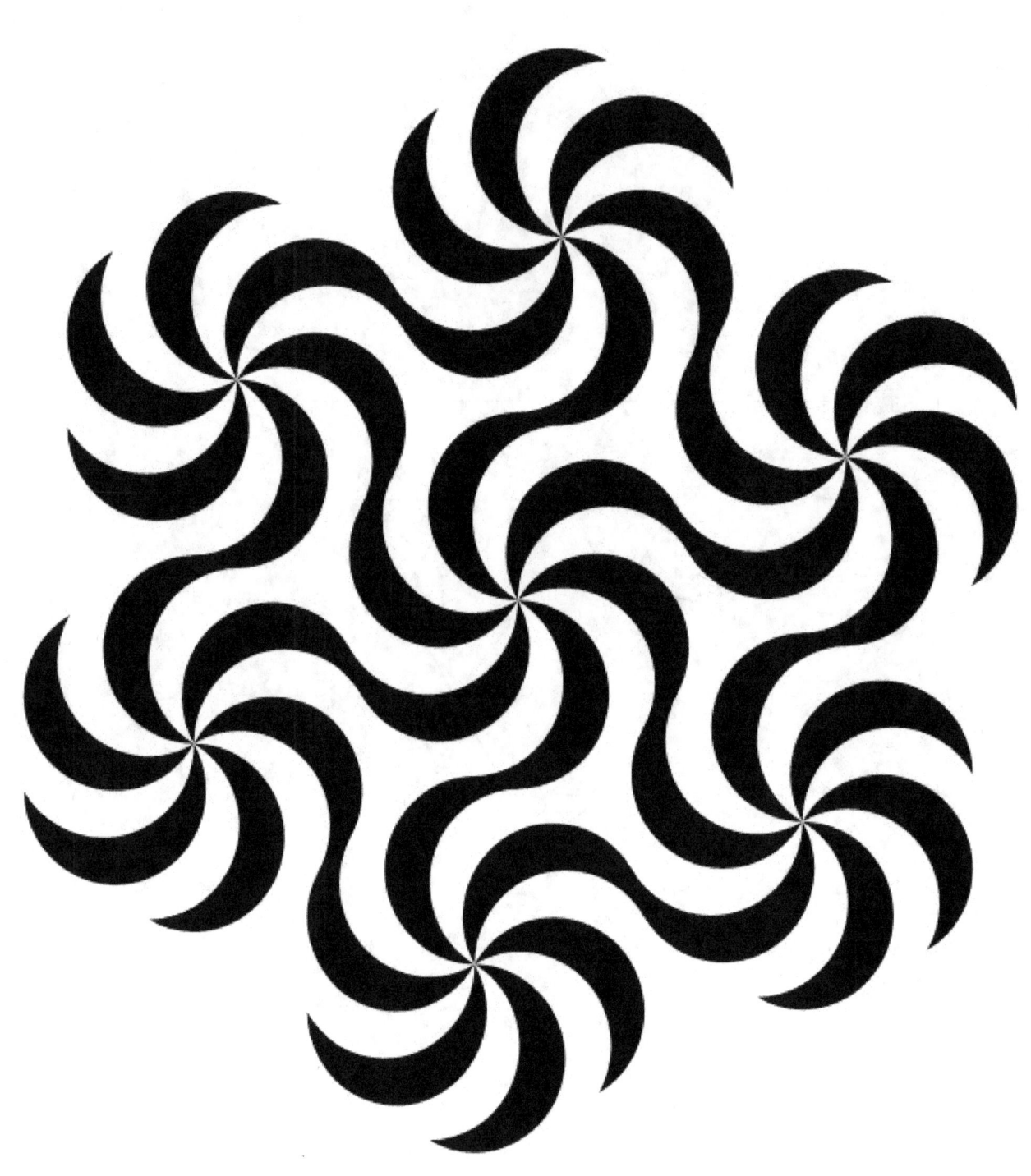

# 20gon Triangles

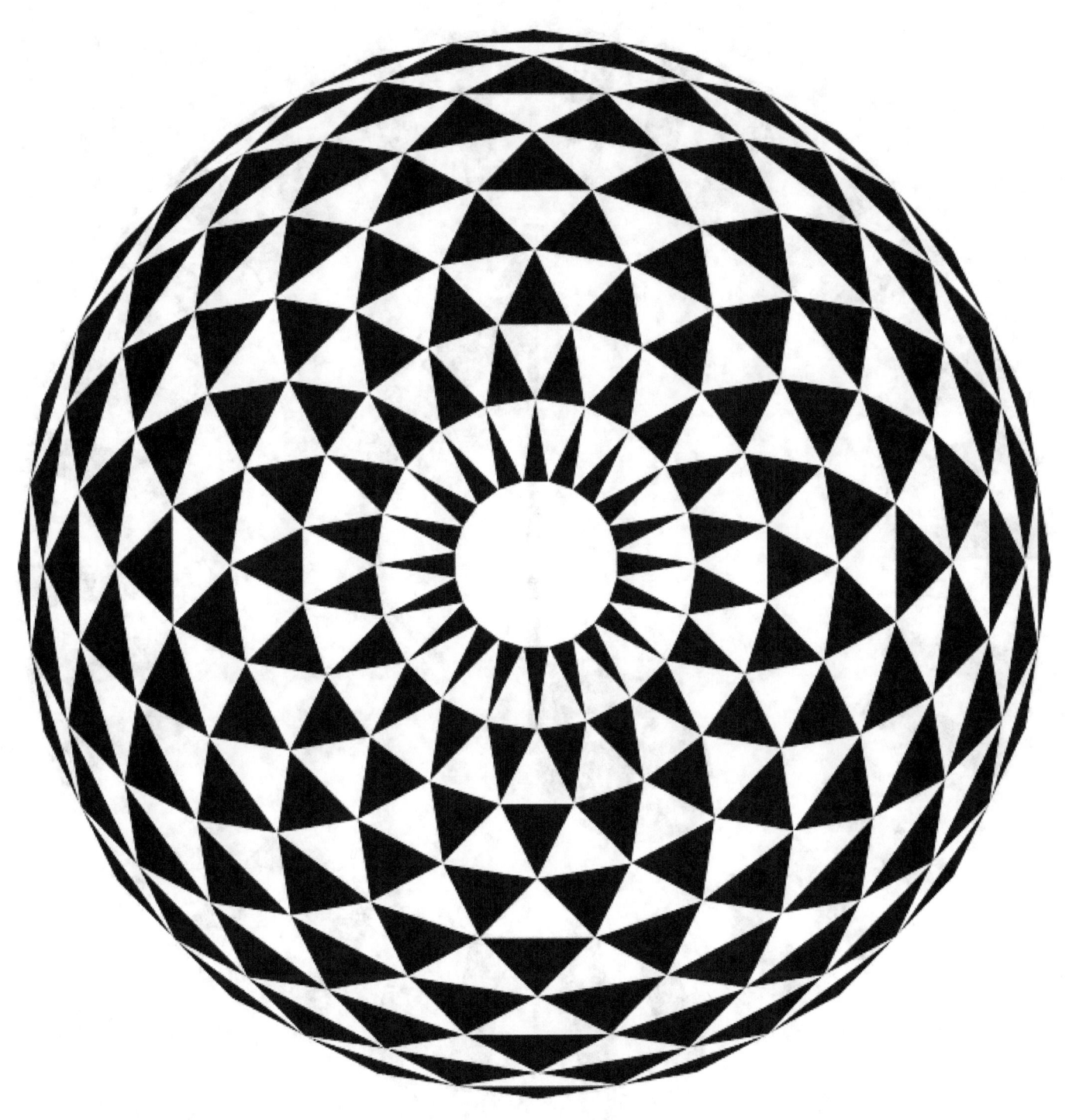

# Music 72gon

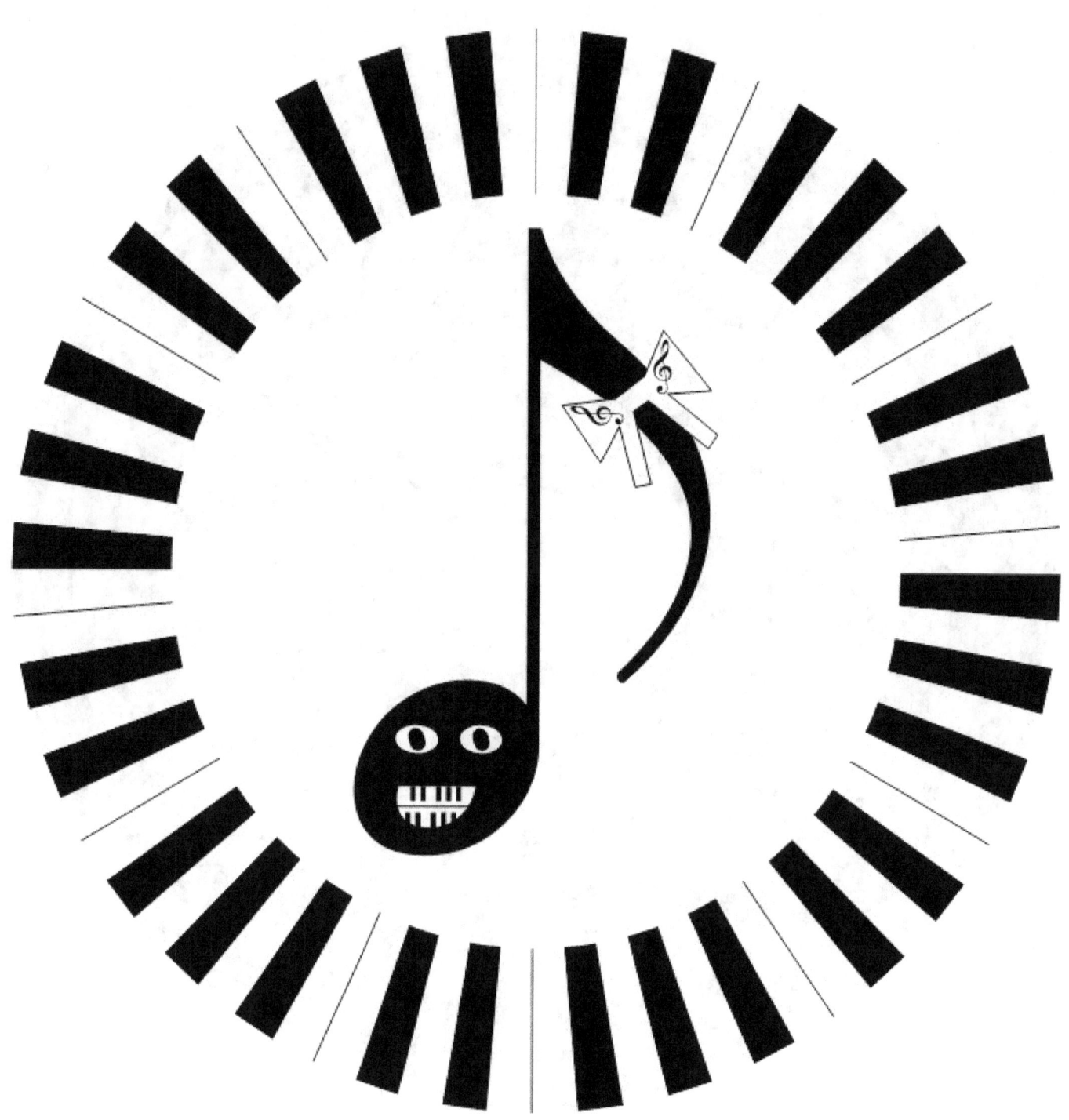

# Stripes Black and White Horizontal

# Stripes Black and White Vertical

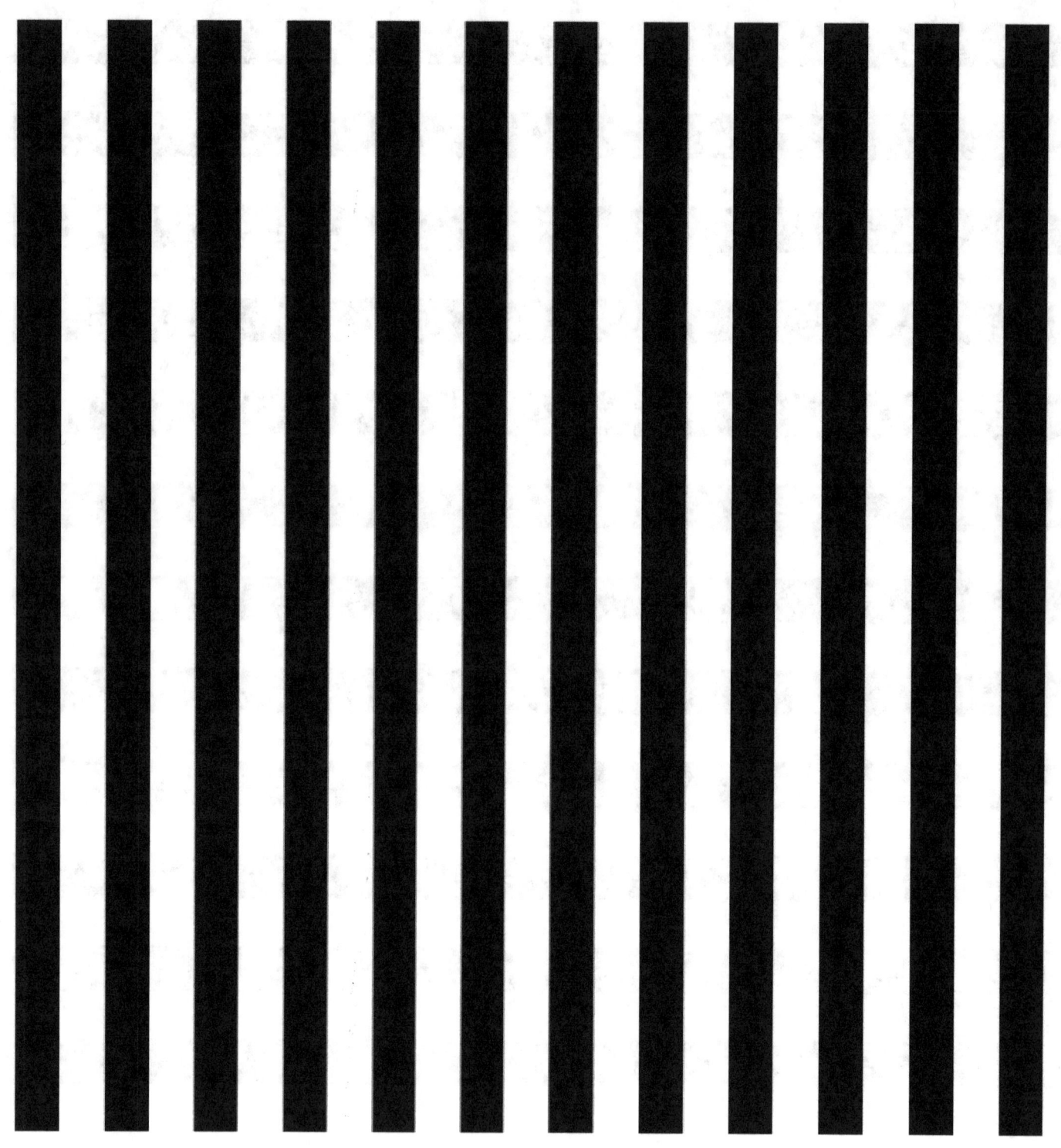

# Stripes Black and White Diagonal

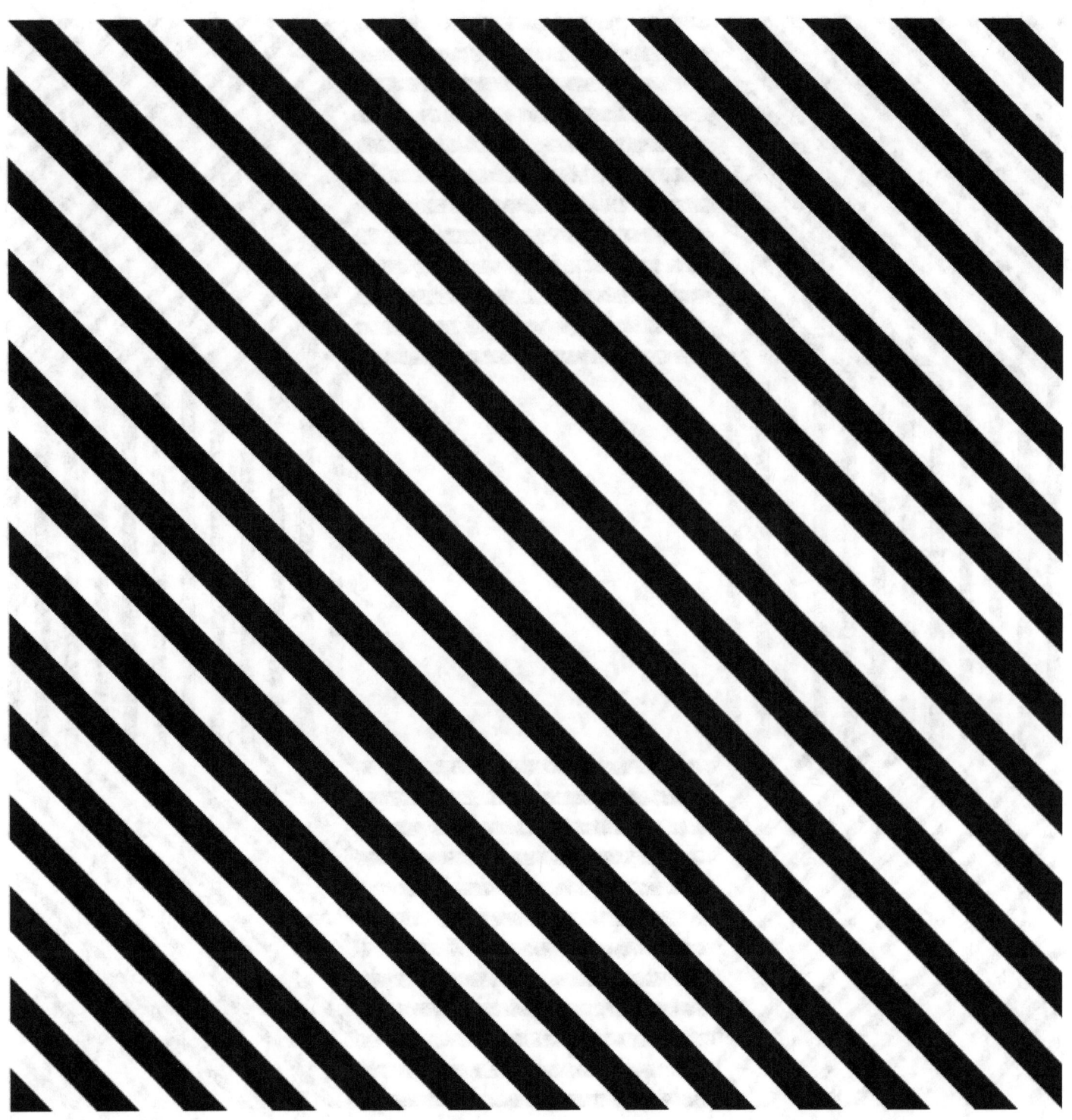

# Stripes Black and White Insanity

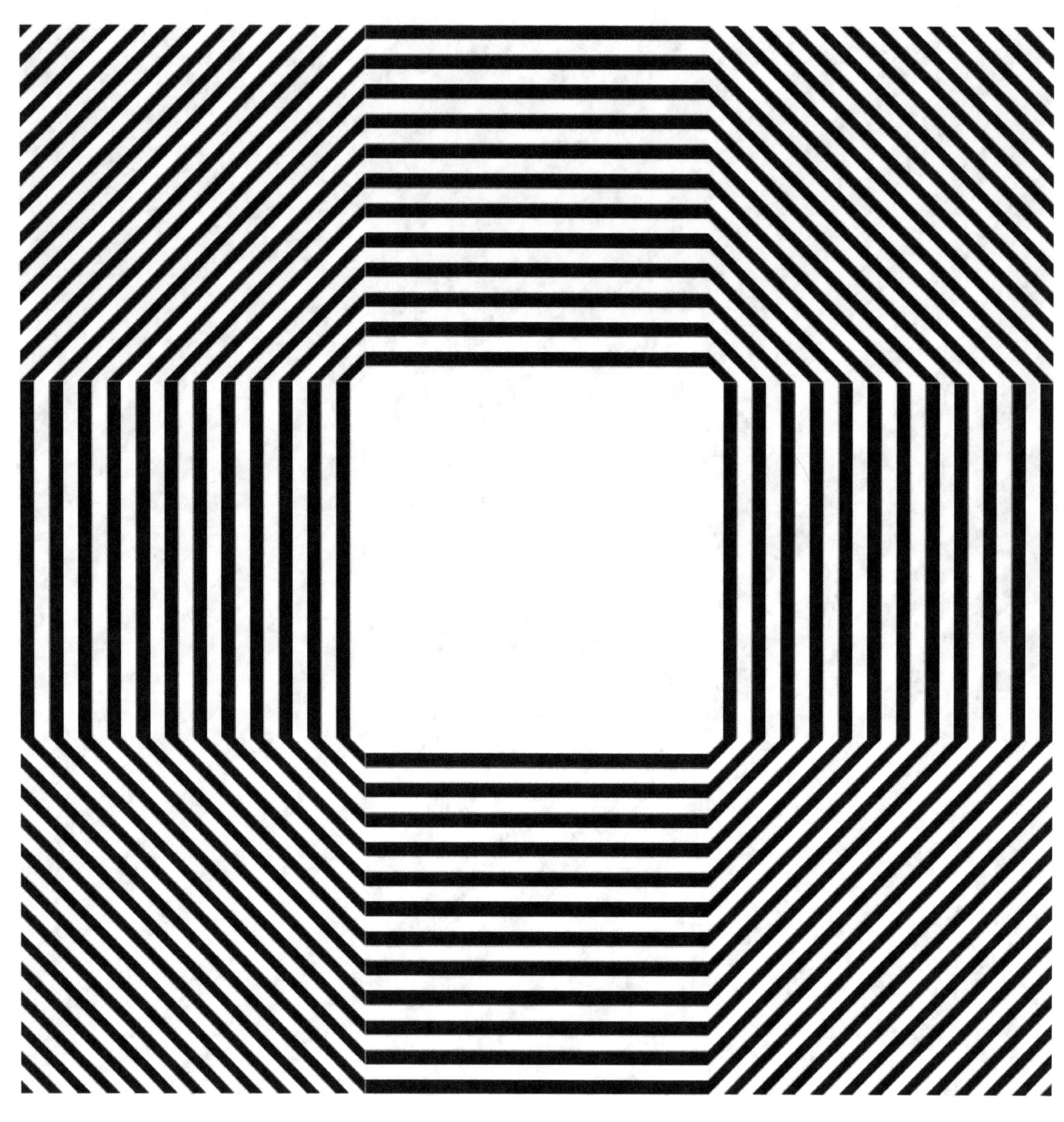

# Happy Cat

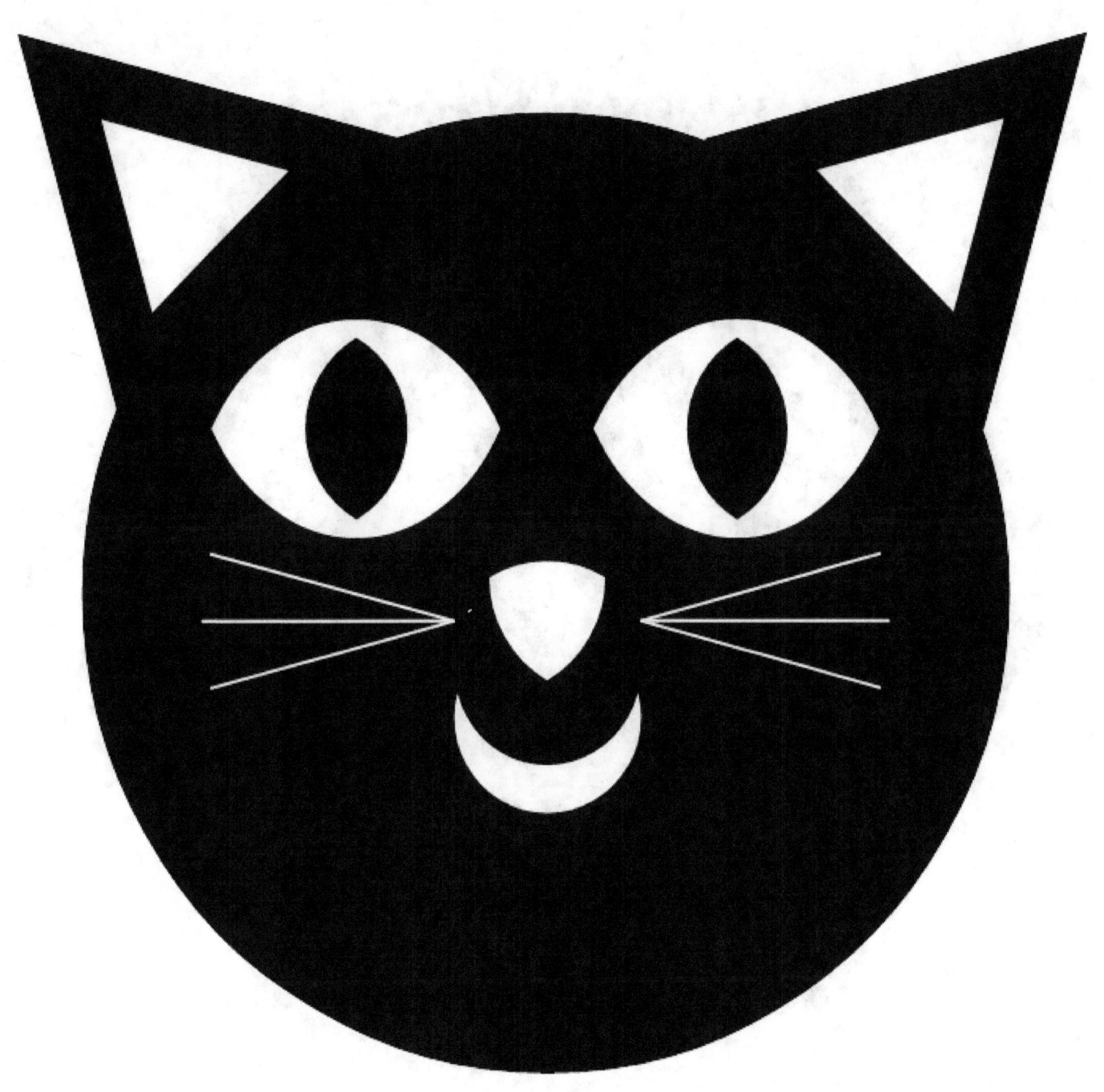

# Hexagon Spiral

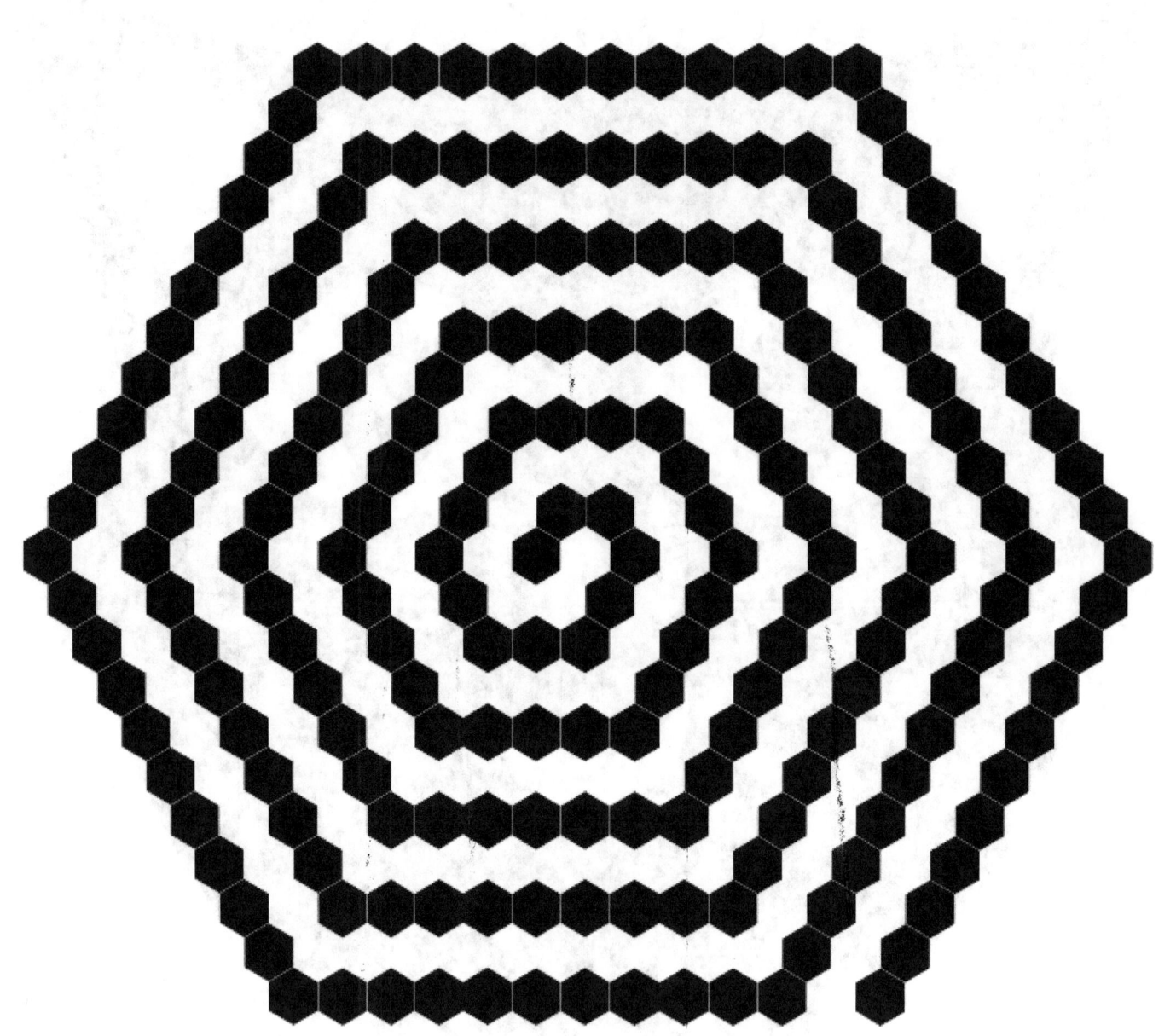

# Triangle Spiral

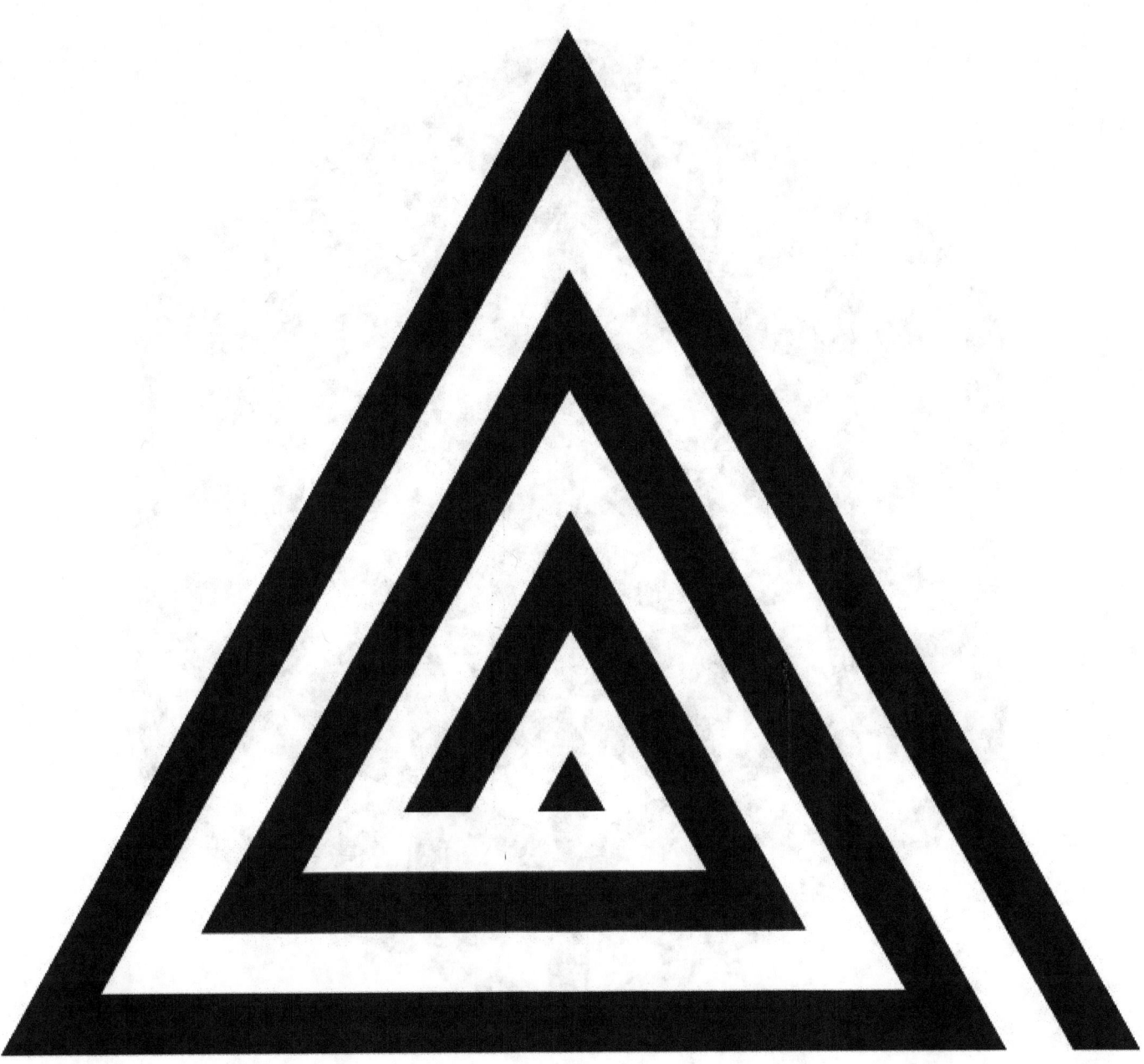

# Flower-of-Life

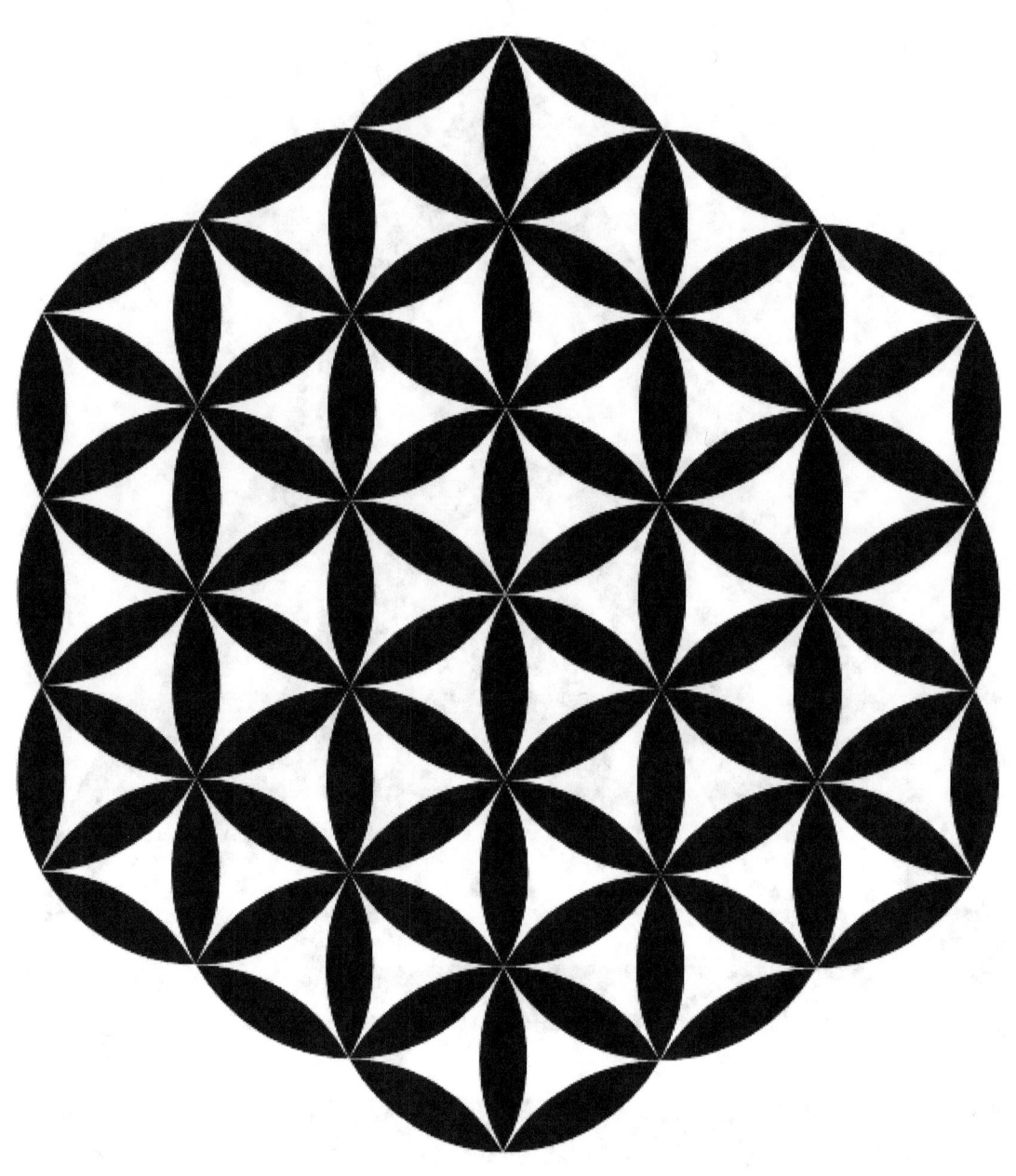

# YinYang

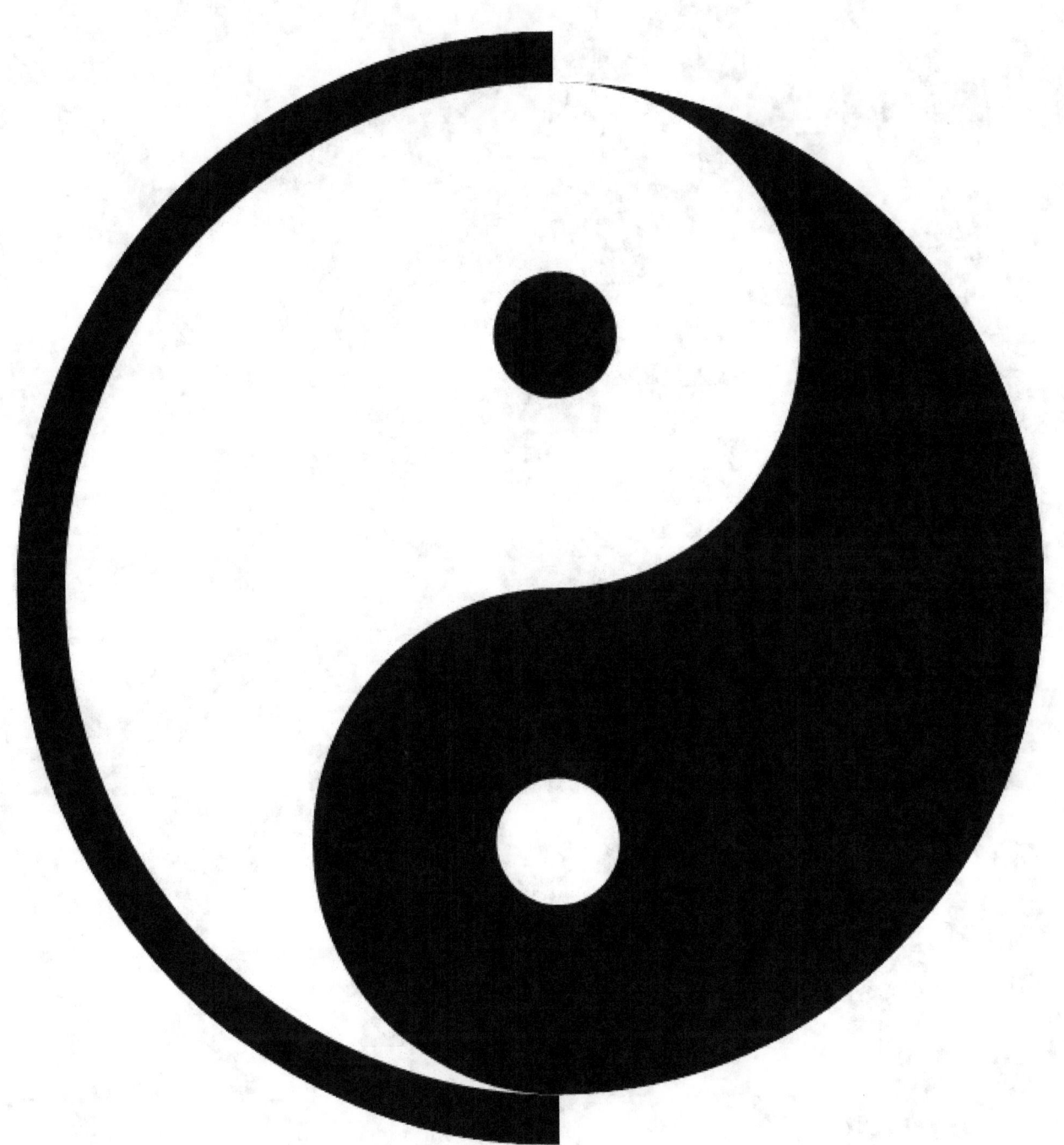

# Black and White Crosses

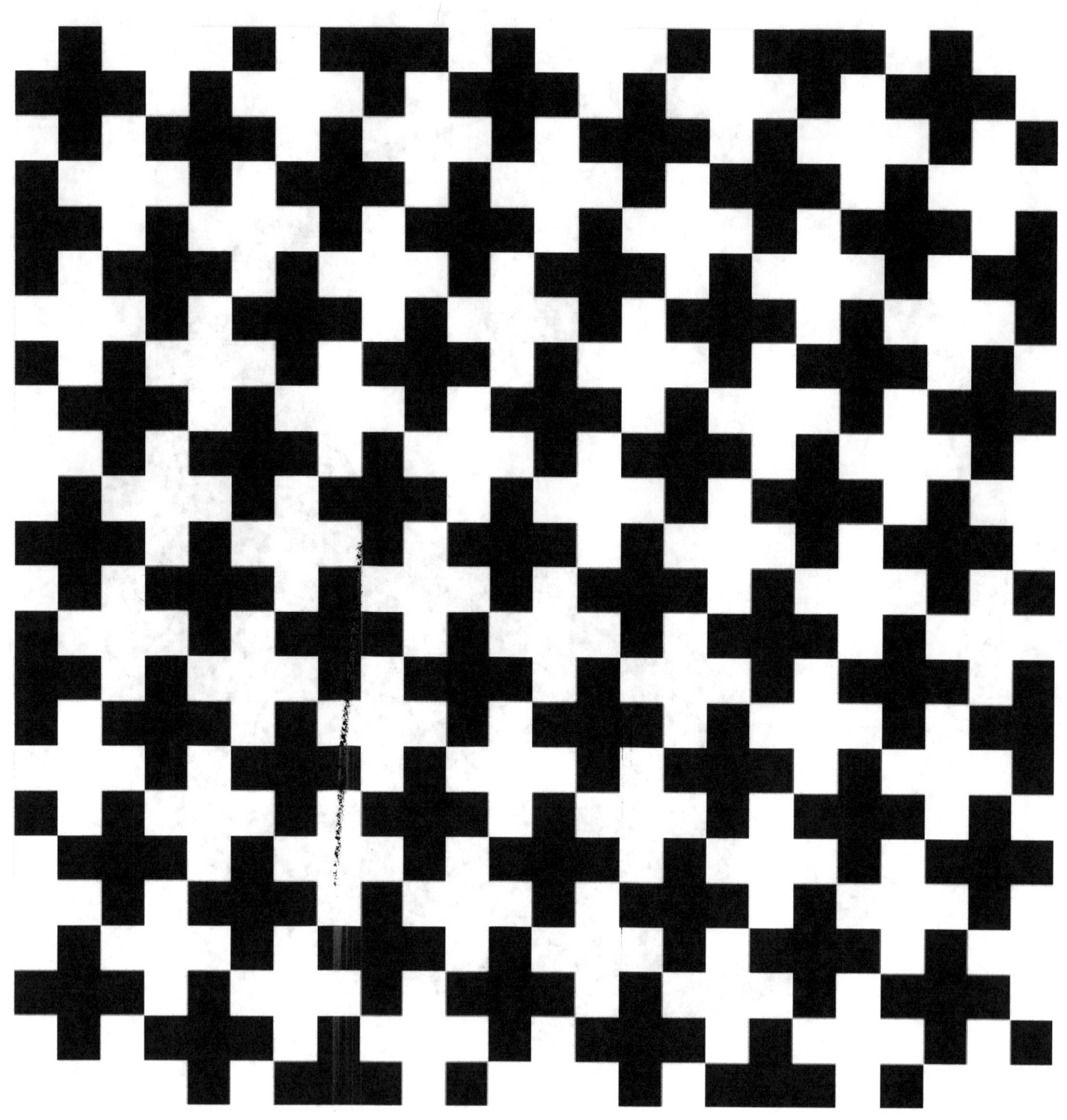

# Triangles in a Square

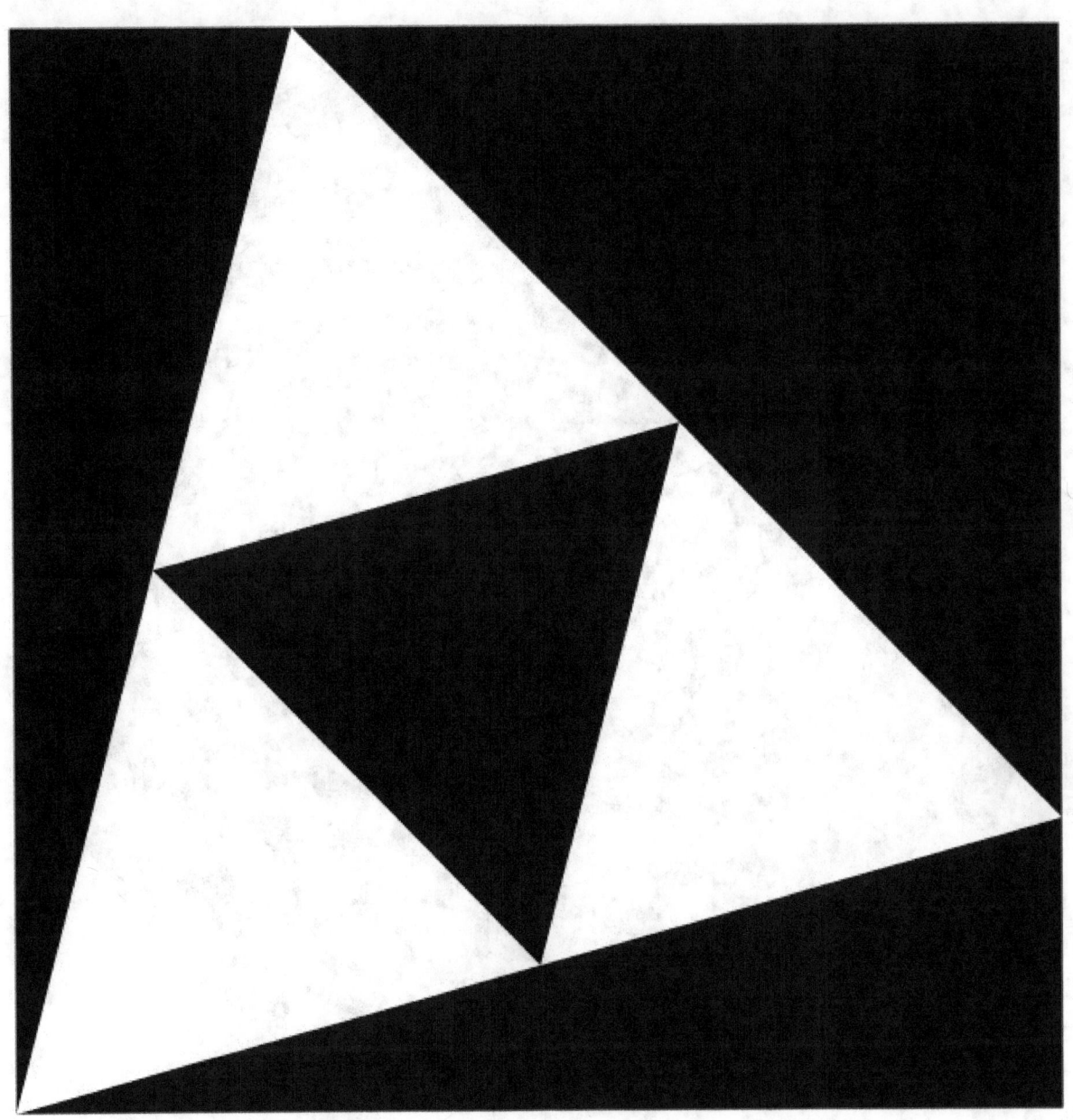

# UV Sphere Top Illusion Black and White

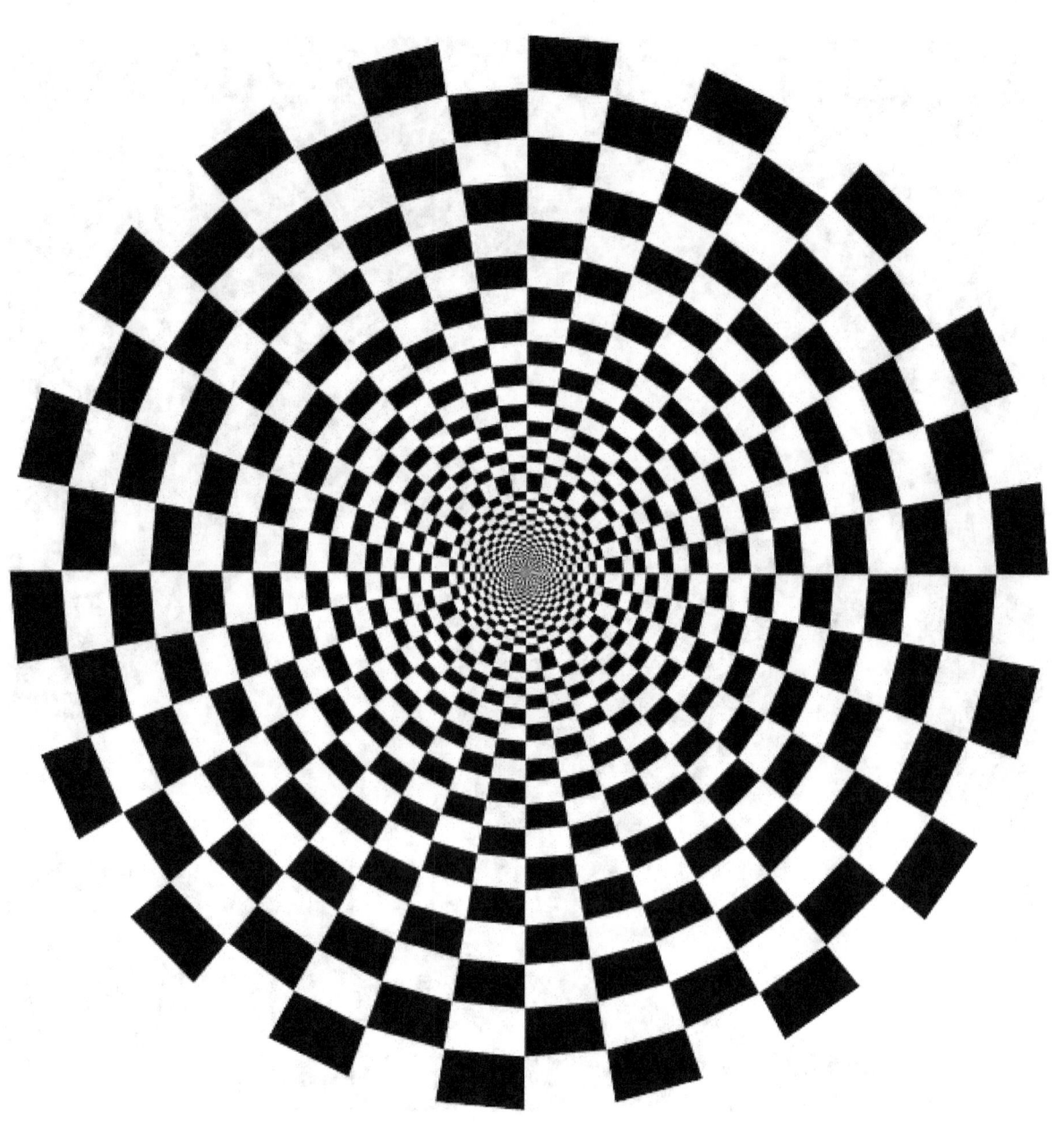

# Octagon Dizziness 23 Stripes

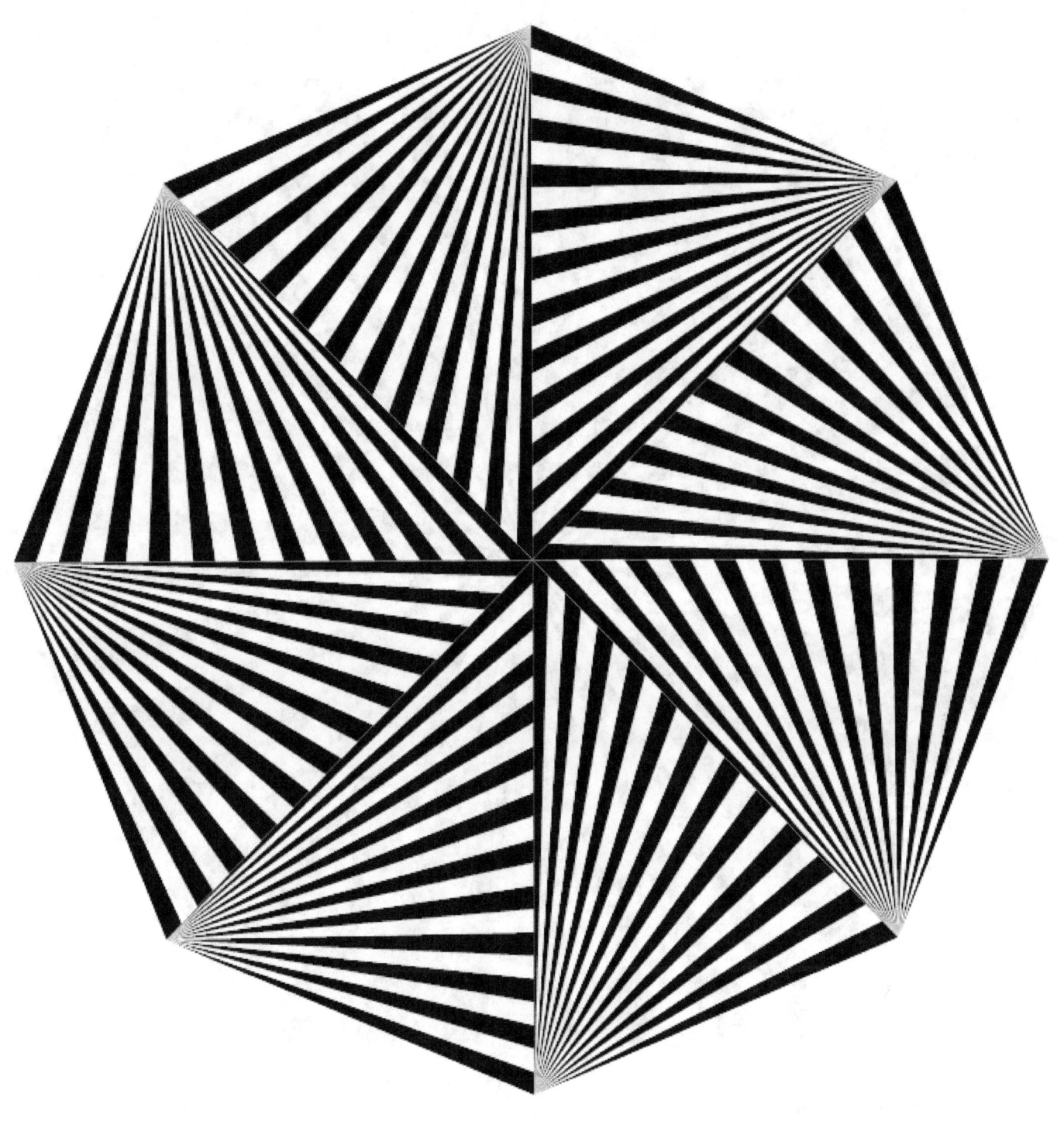

# Black and White Hexagon 72 Stripes

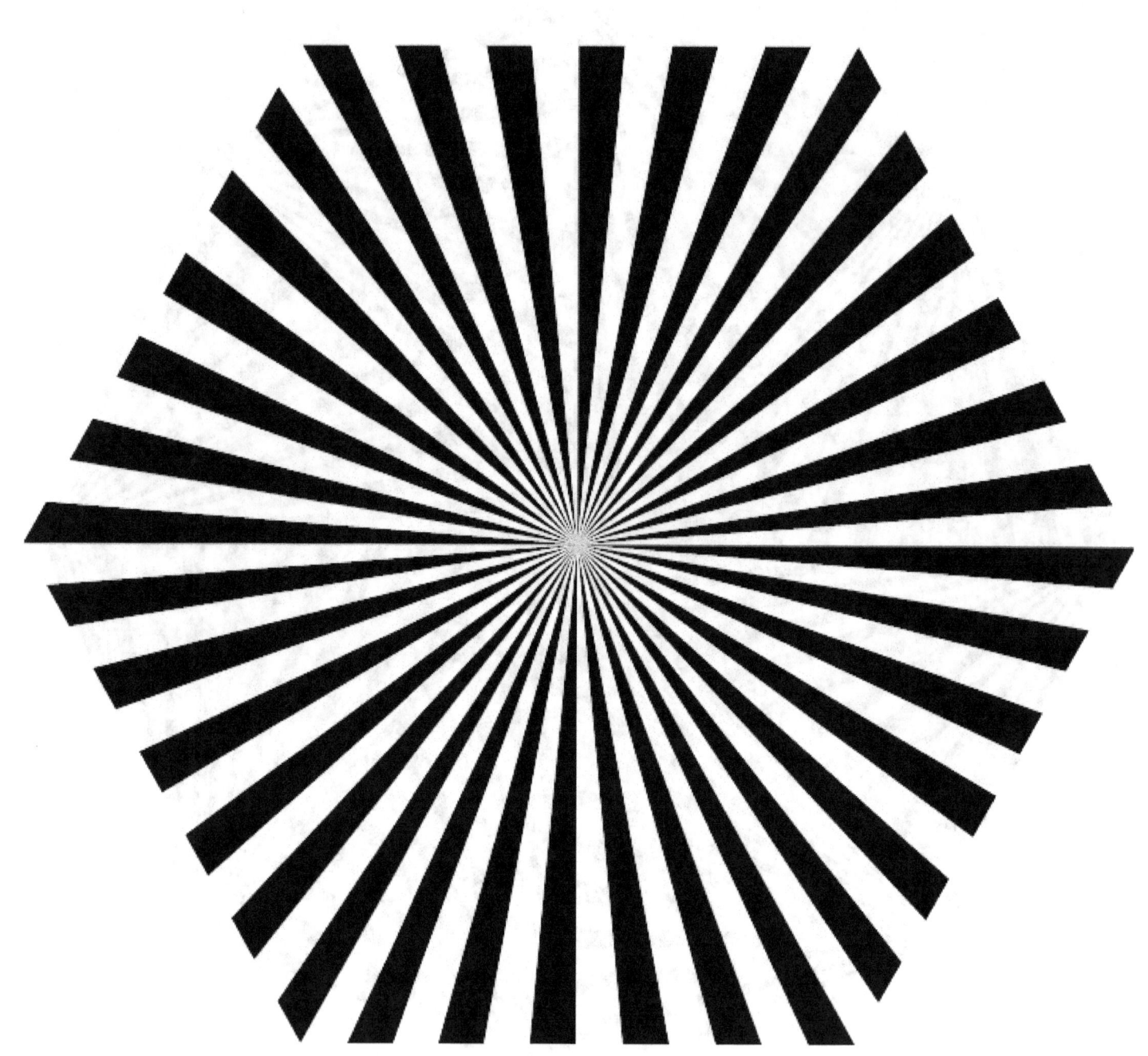

# 2 Color Square Spiral

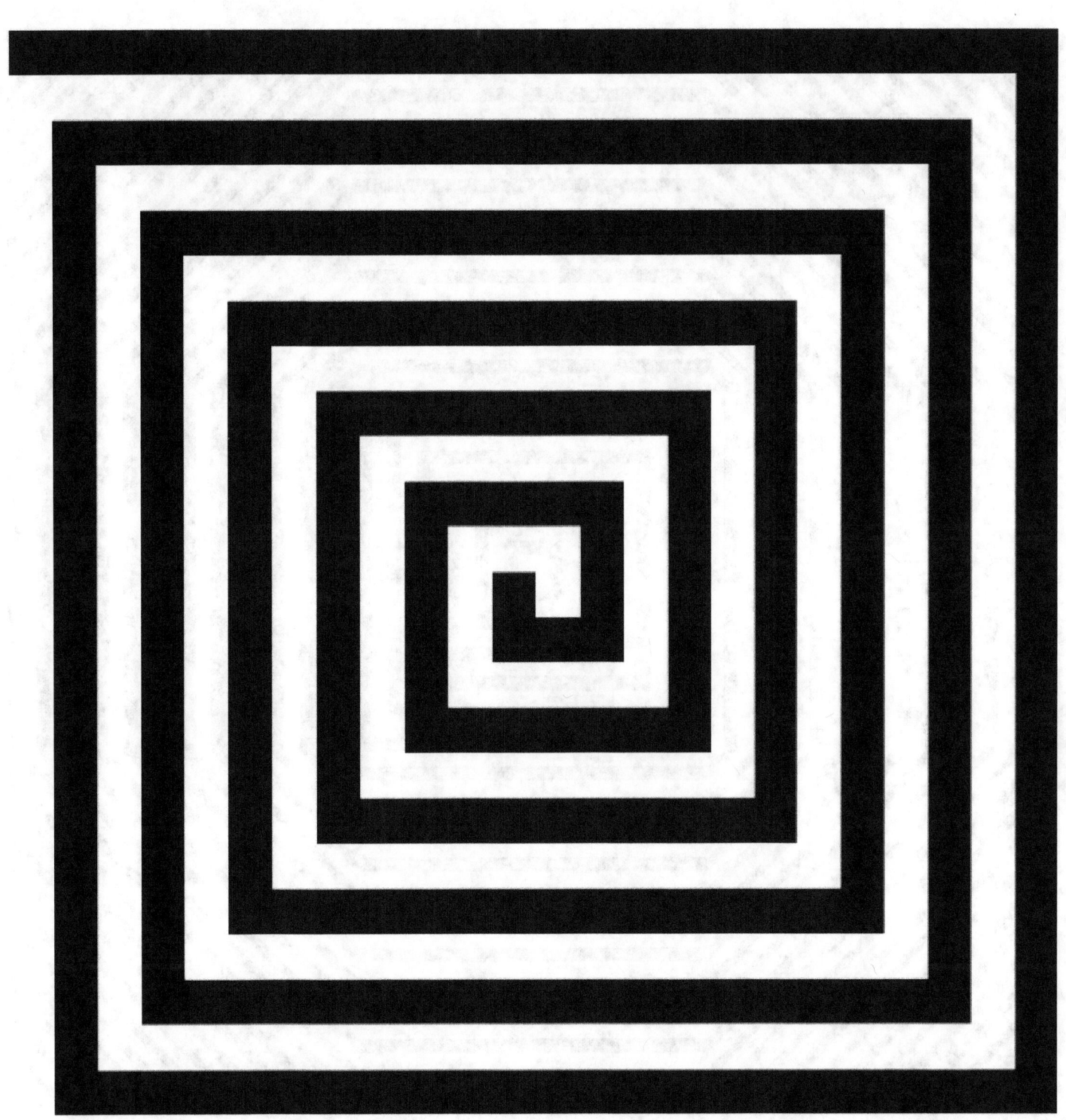

# Insane Stripes Remix

# Insane Stripes Remix 2

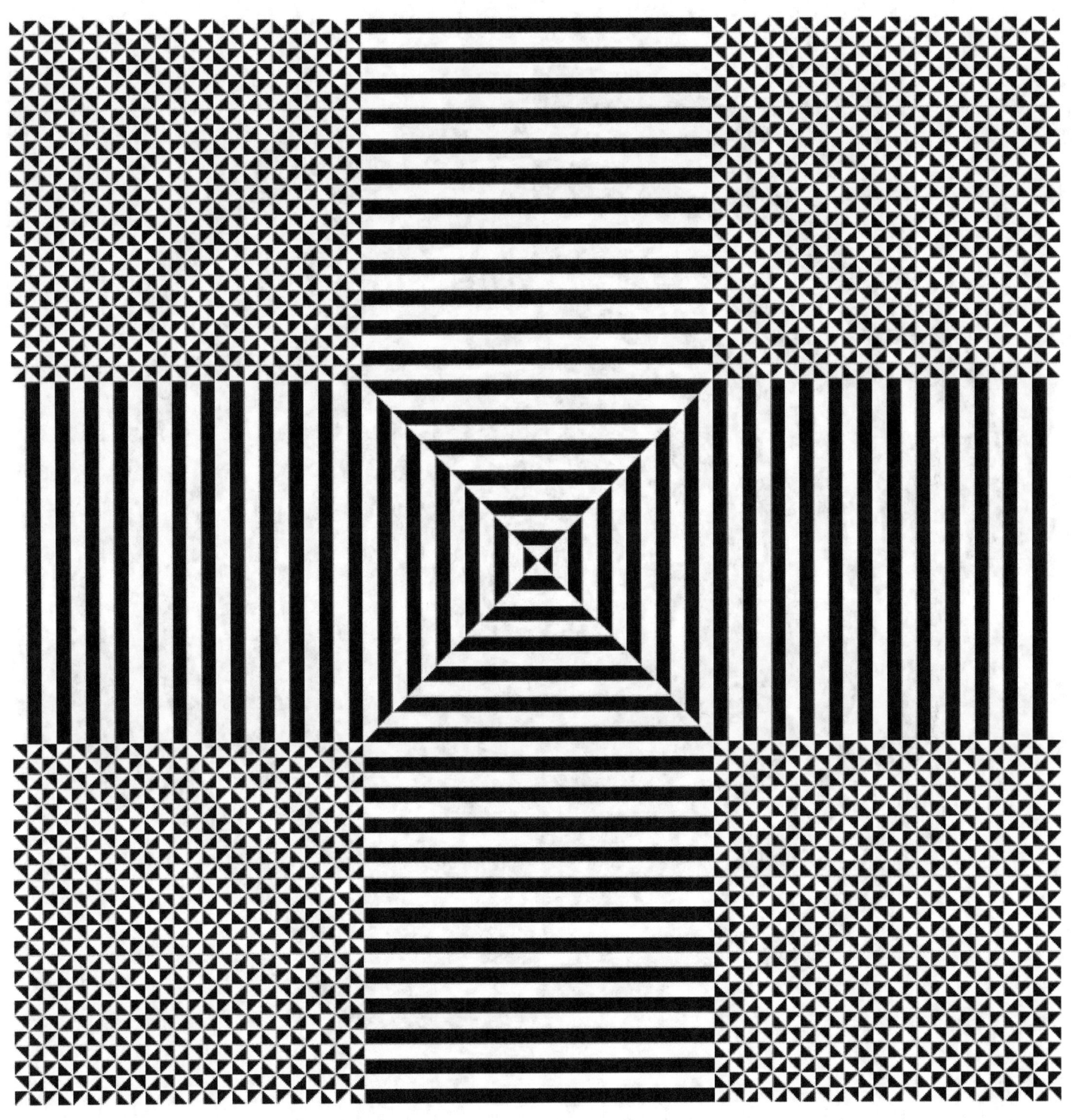

# Sliced Circle Target

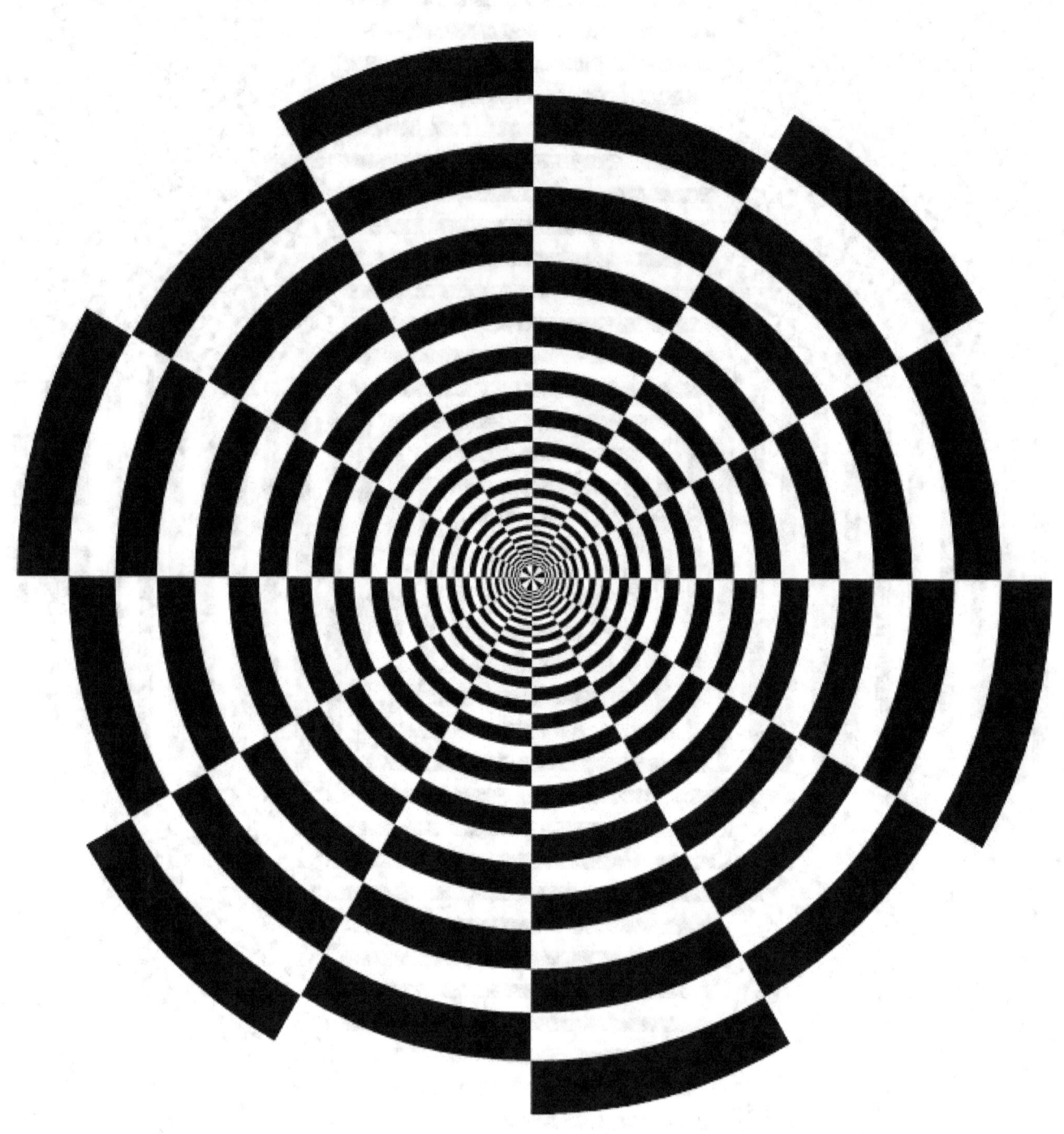

# Insane Stripes Remix 3

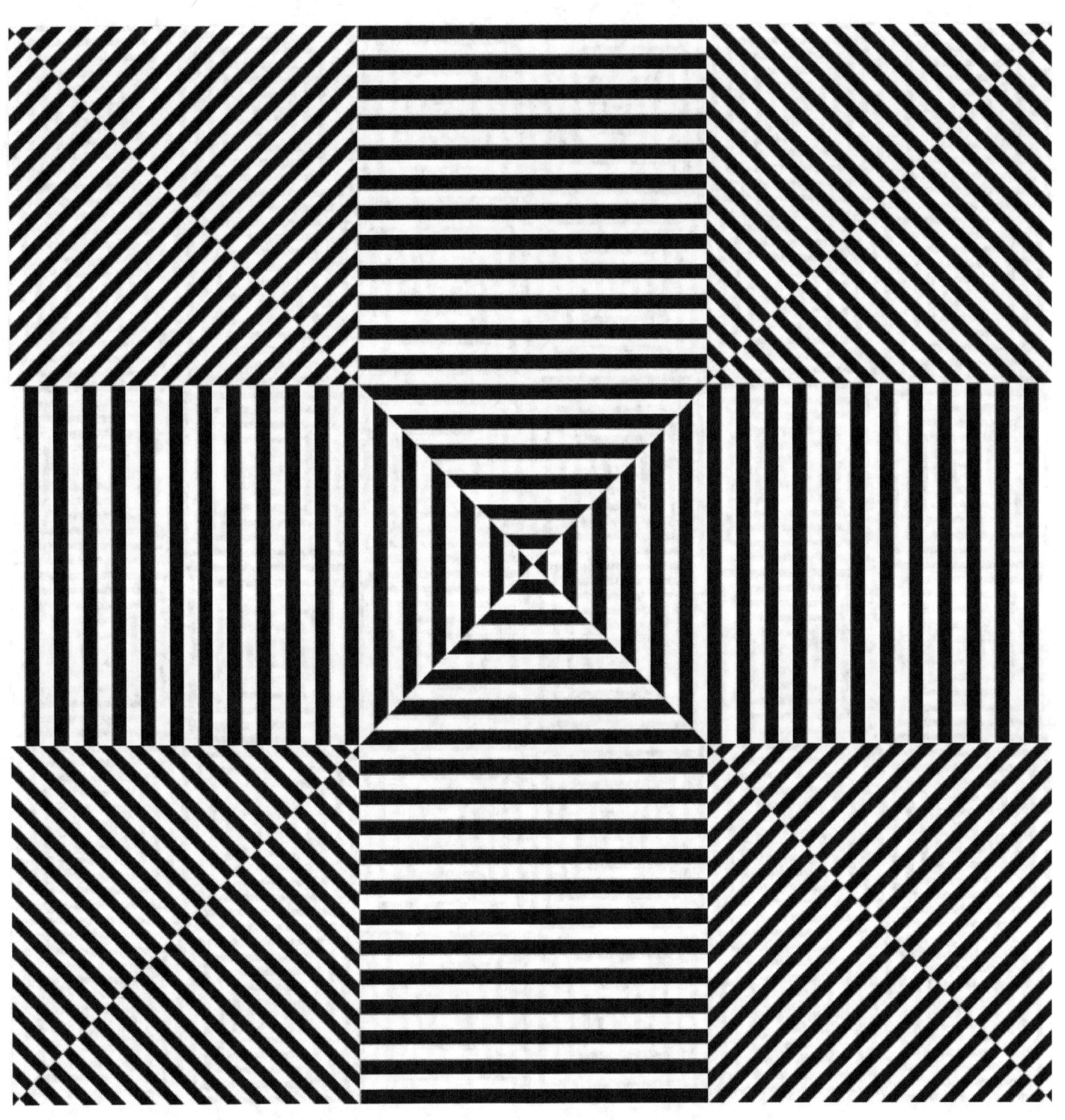

# Dizzy Zebra Thoughts

# Dizzy Zebra Thoughts 2

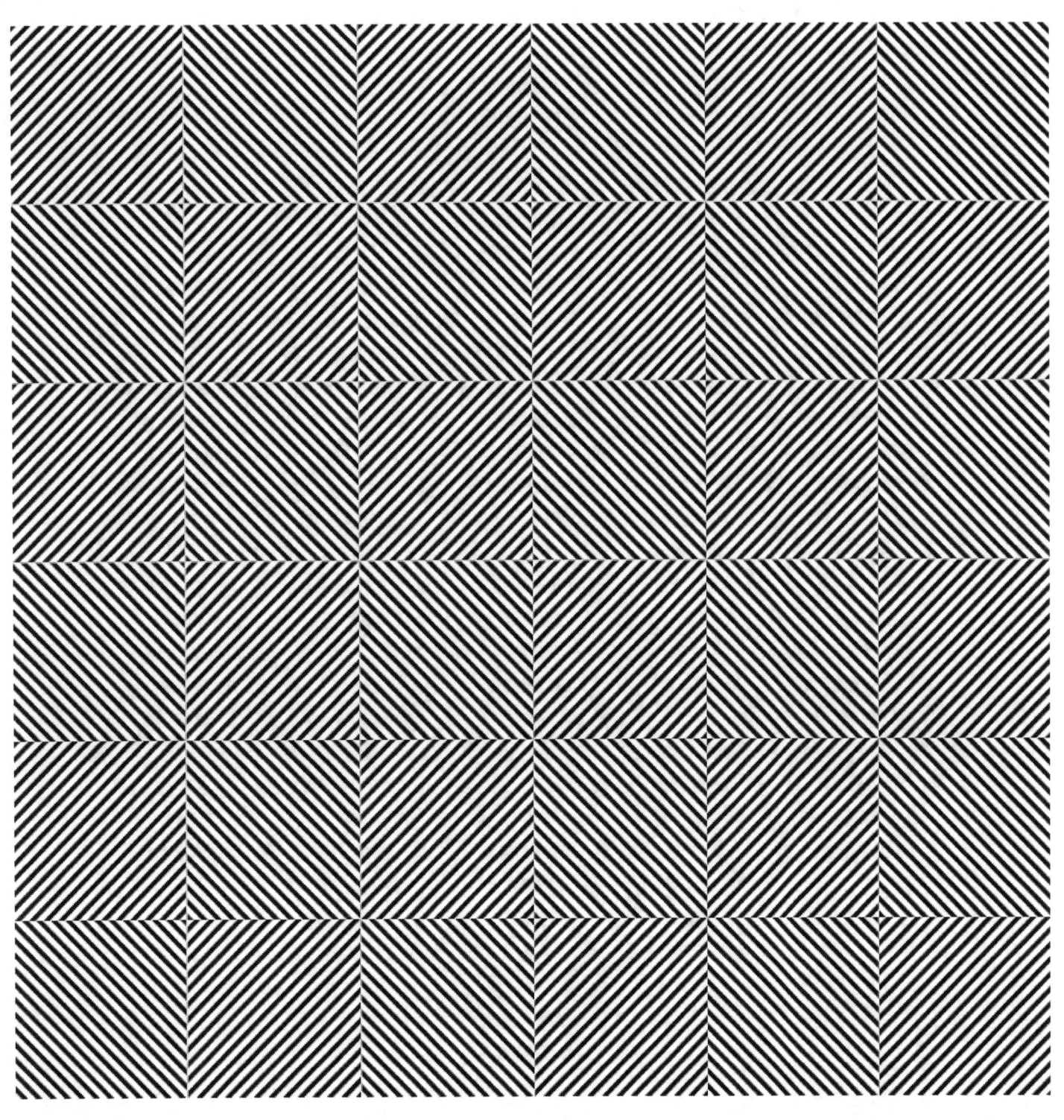

# Striped Triangles Horizontal

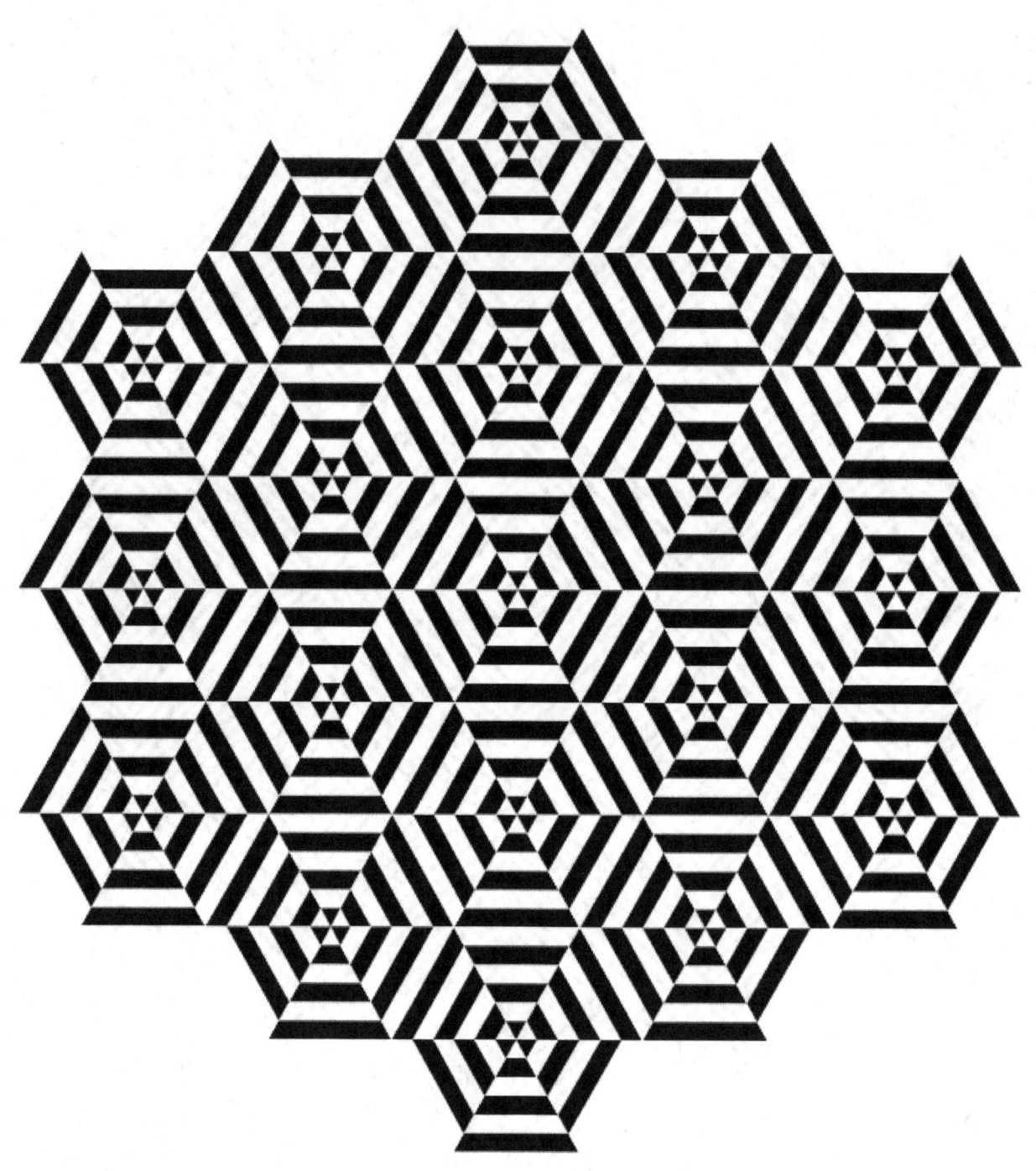

# Striped Hexagons Horizontal

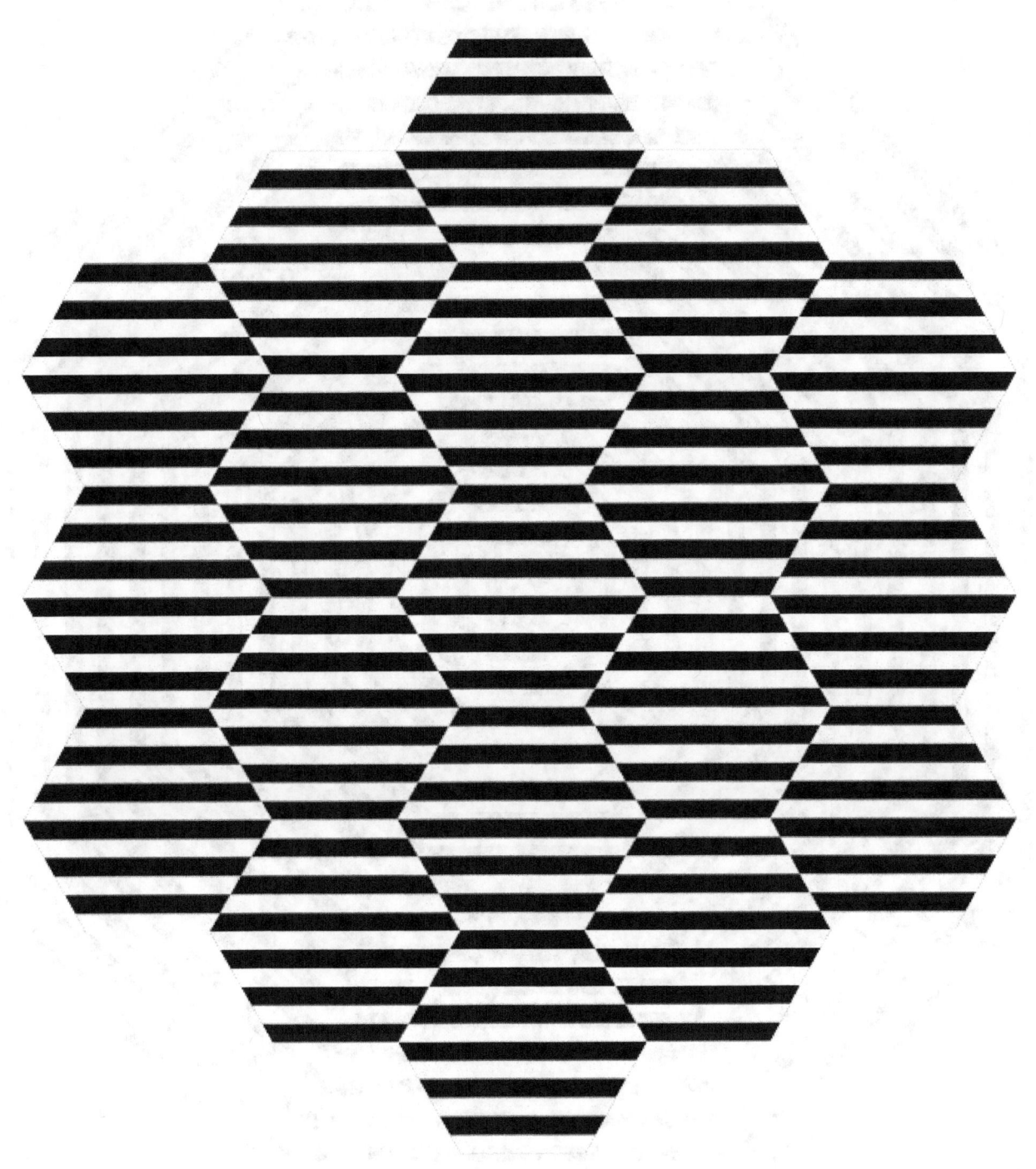

# Octagon Stripe Madness

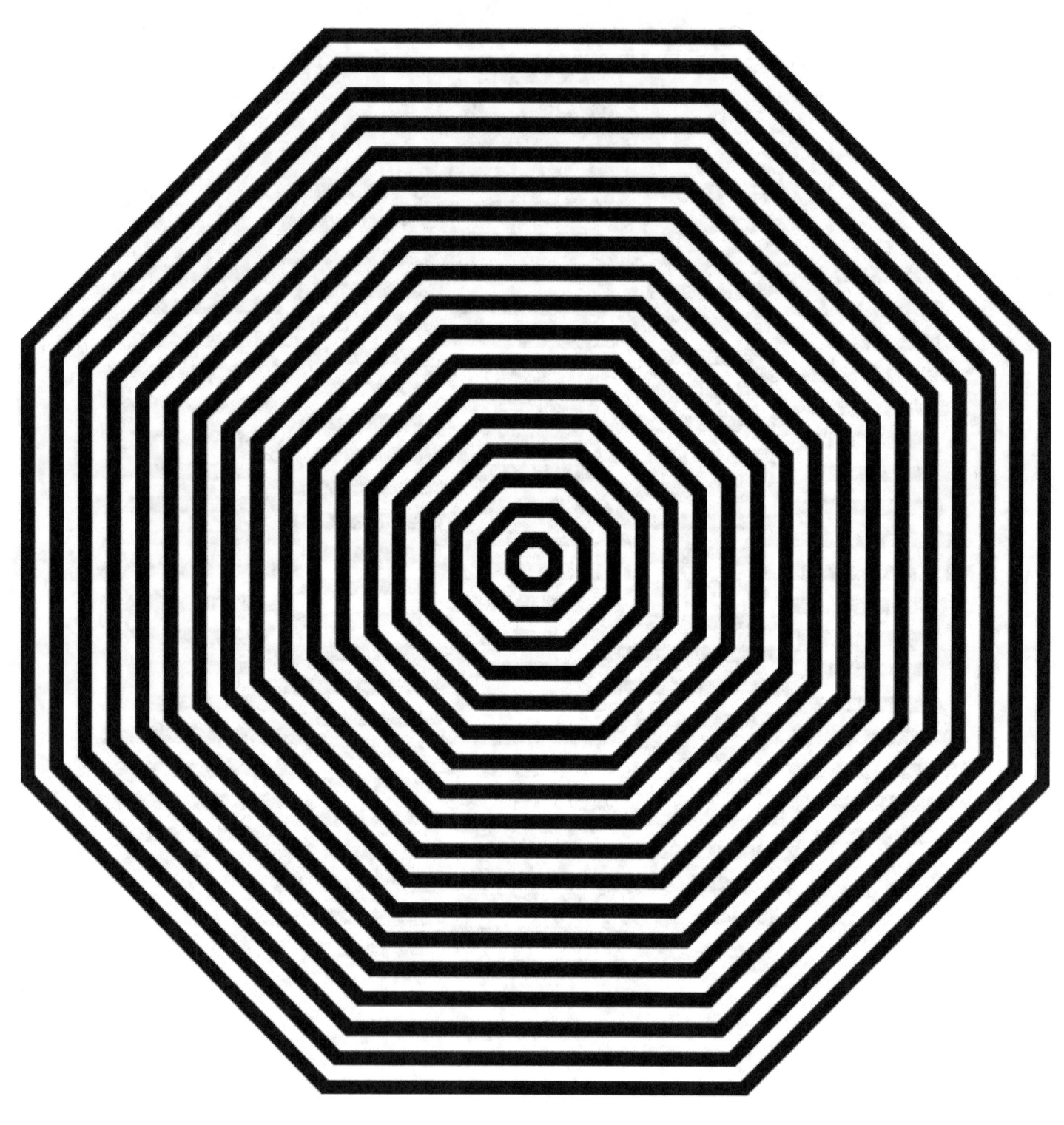

# Octagon Stripe Madness Remix

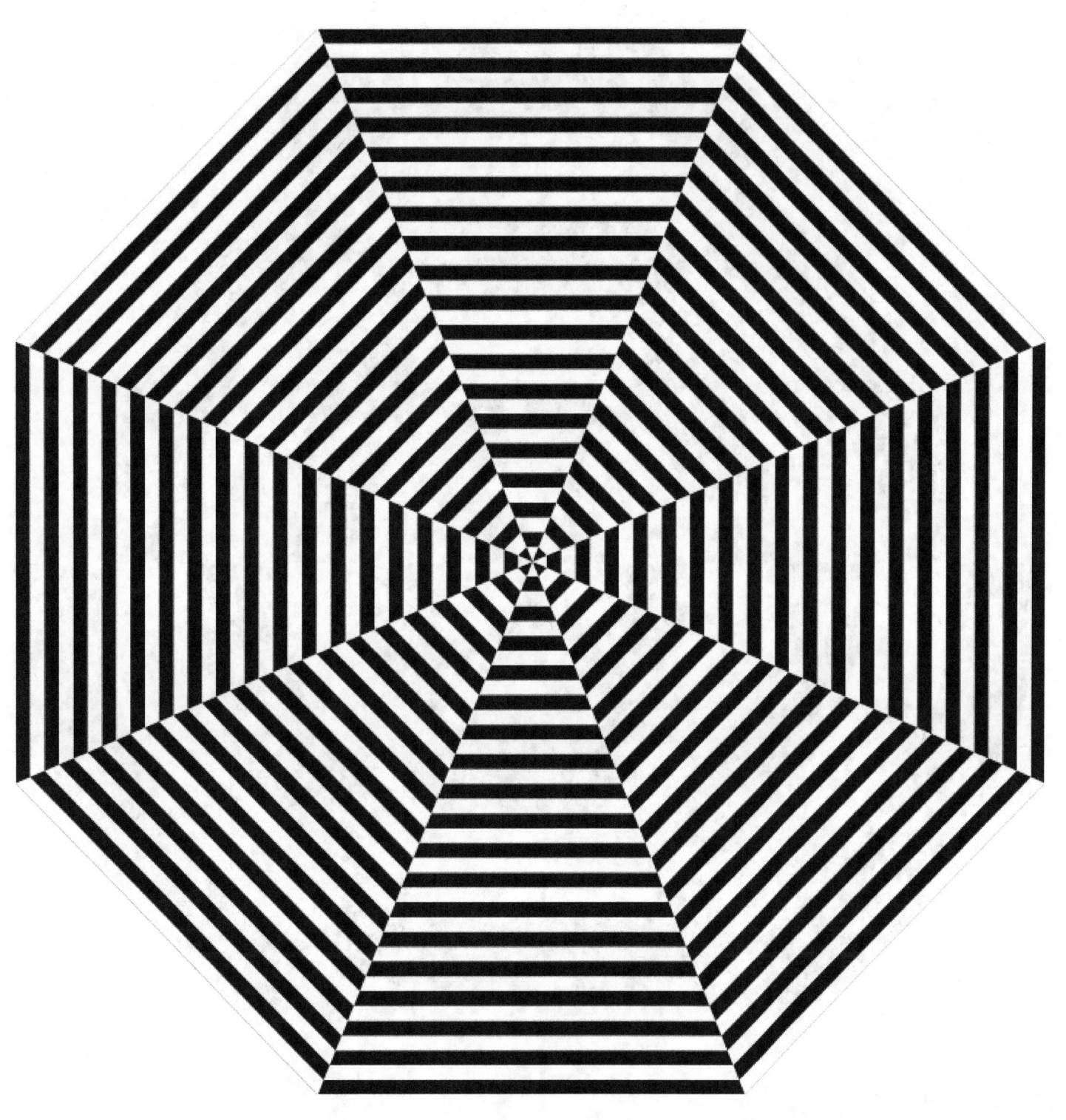

# Circle Black White Sliced

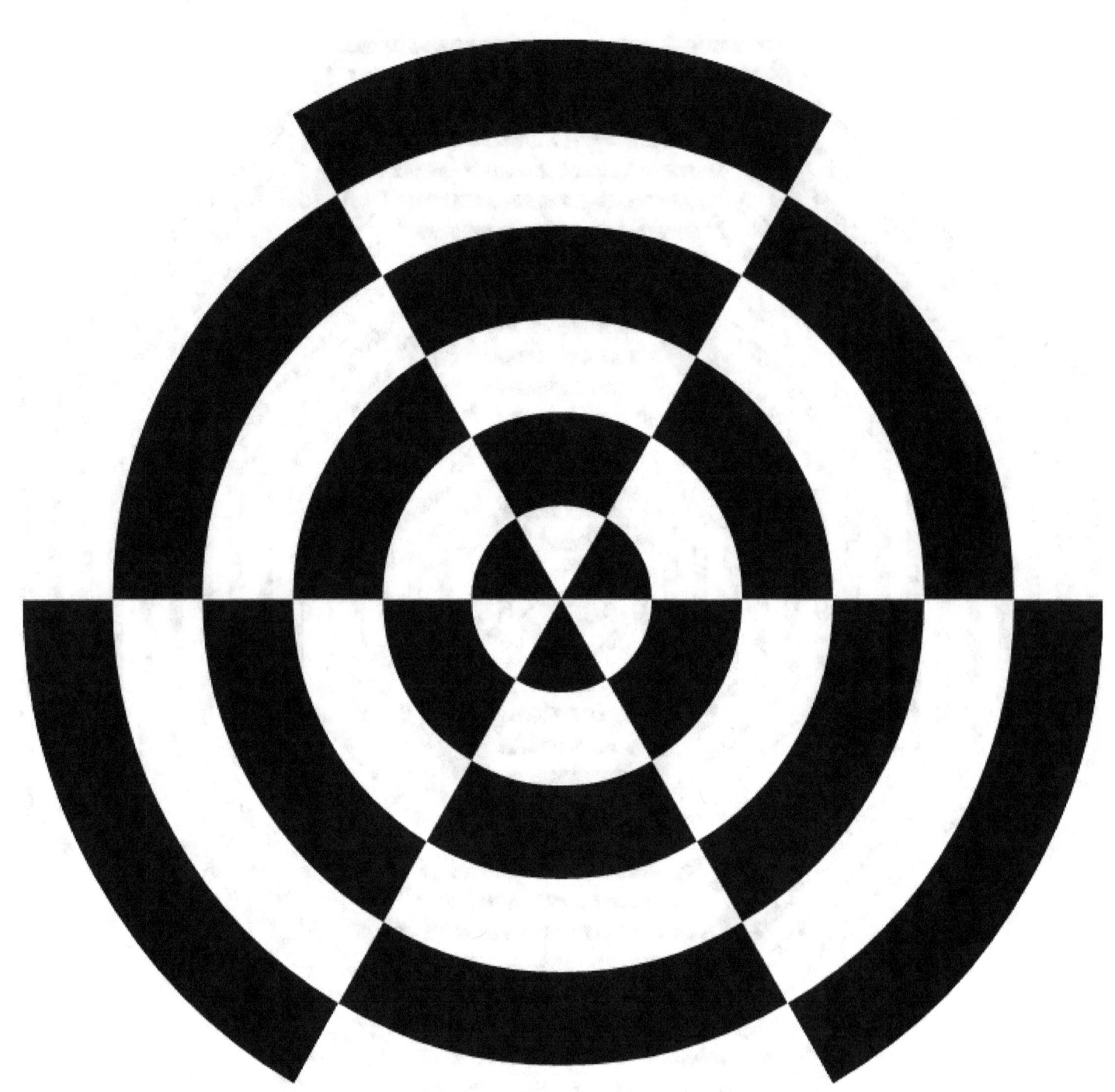

# Triangle Black White Hexagon

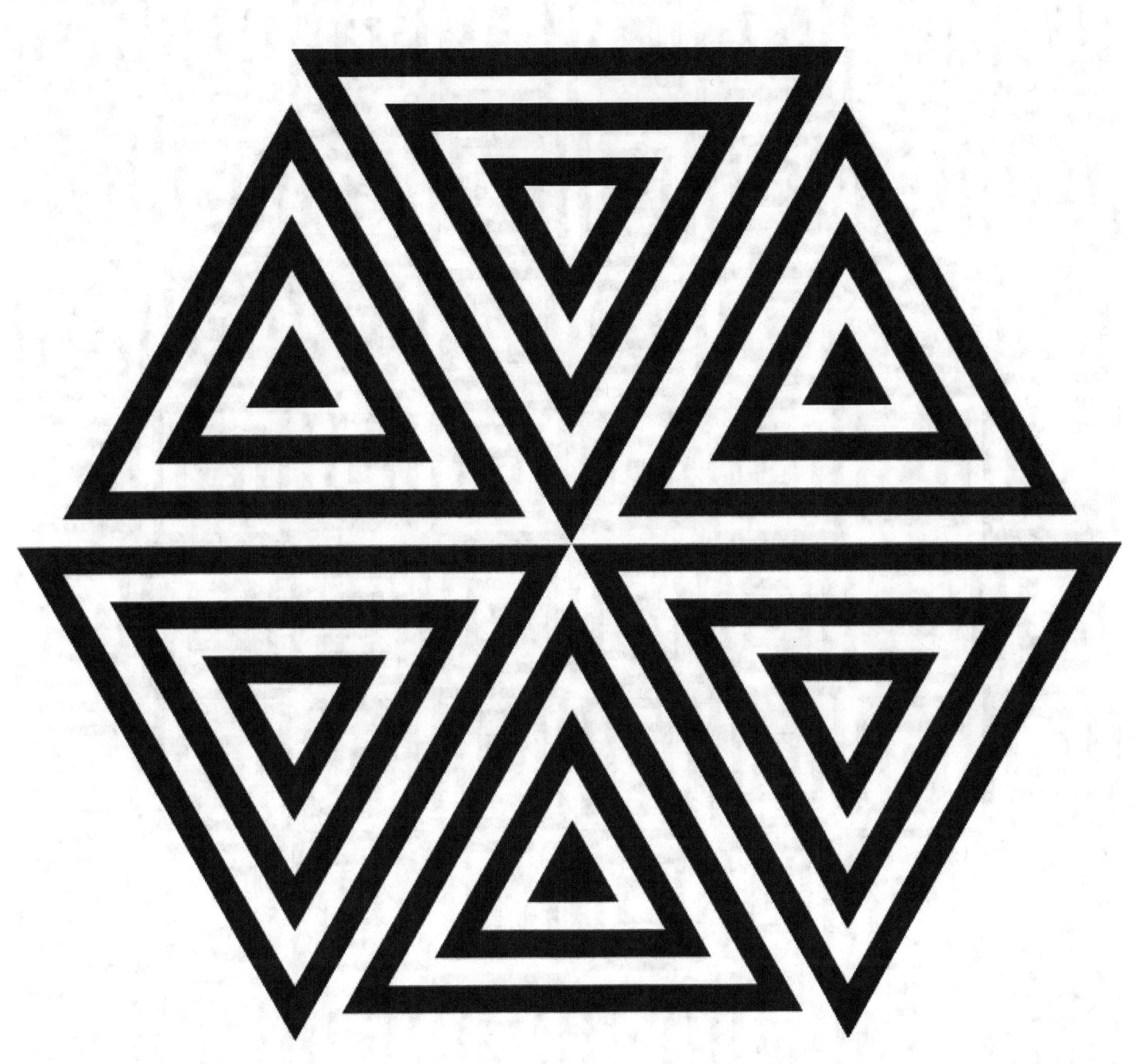

# Square Target 8x8 Chessboard

# Triangular Polka Dots Black on White

# Triangular Polka Dots White on Black

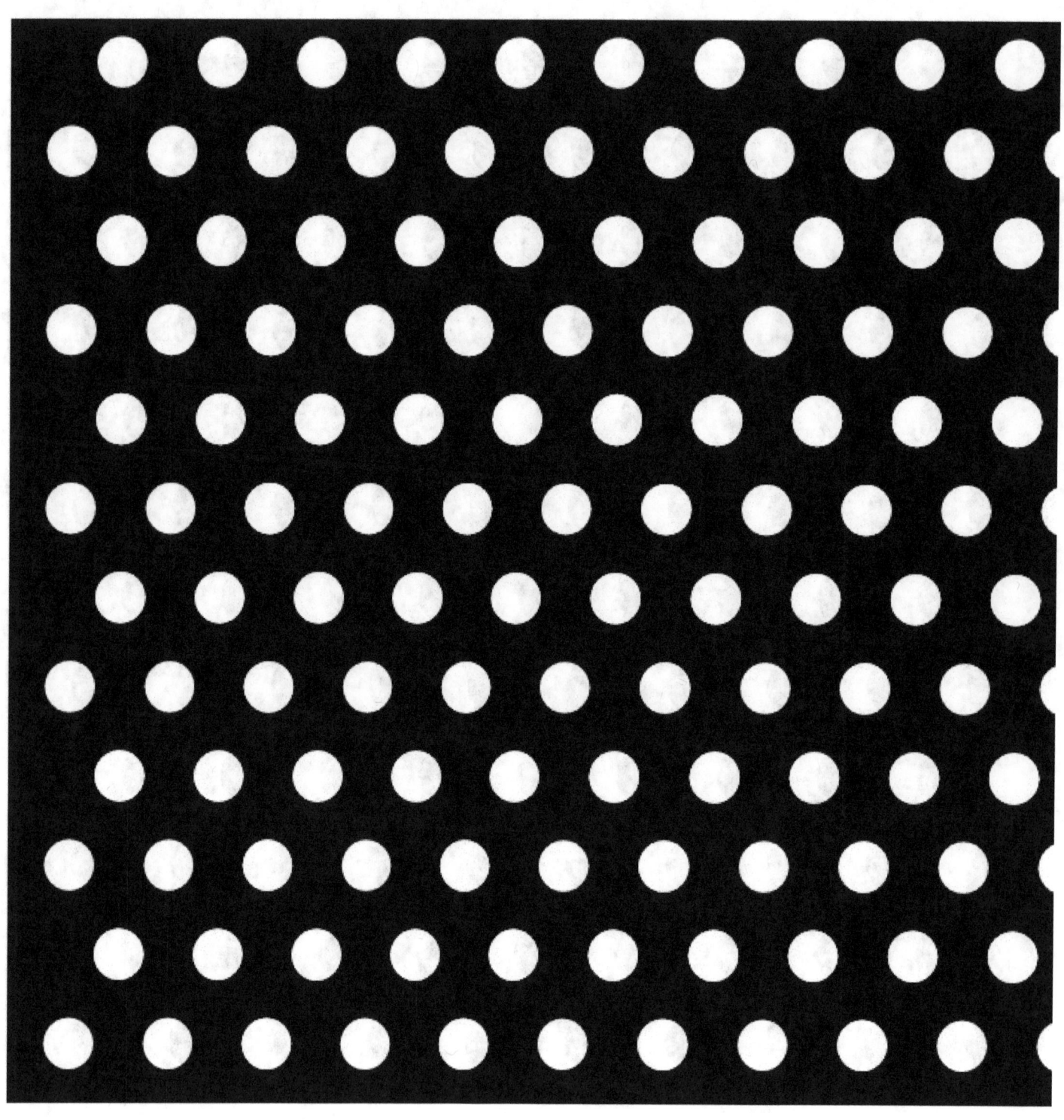

# Spaced 6 Petal Flowers Black on White

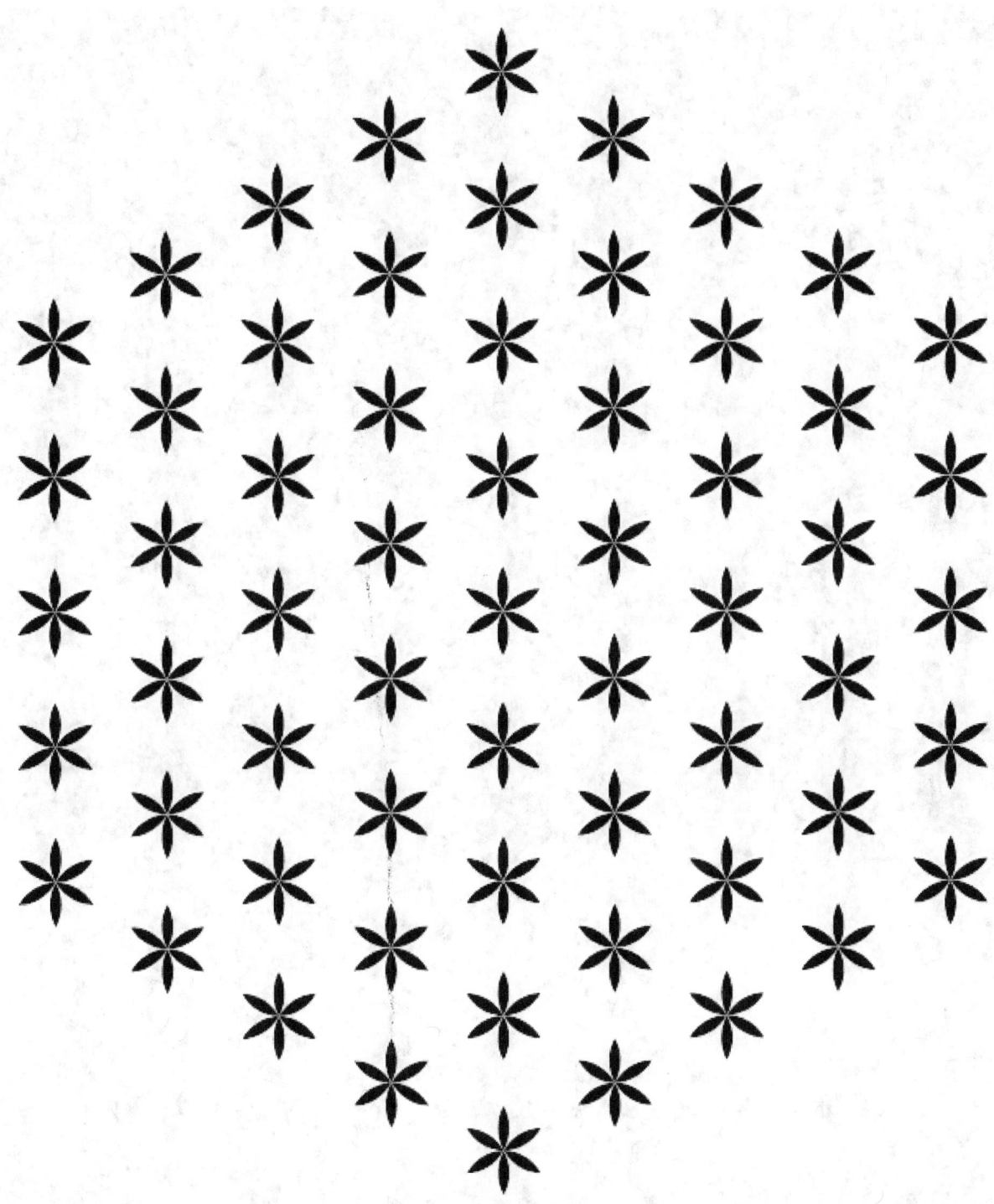

# Spaced 6 Petal Flowers White on Black

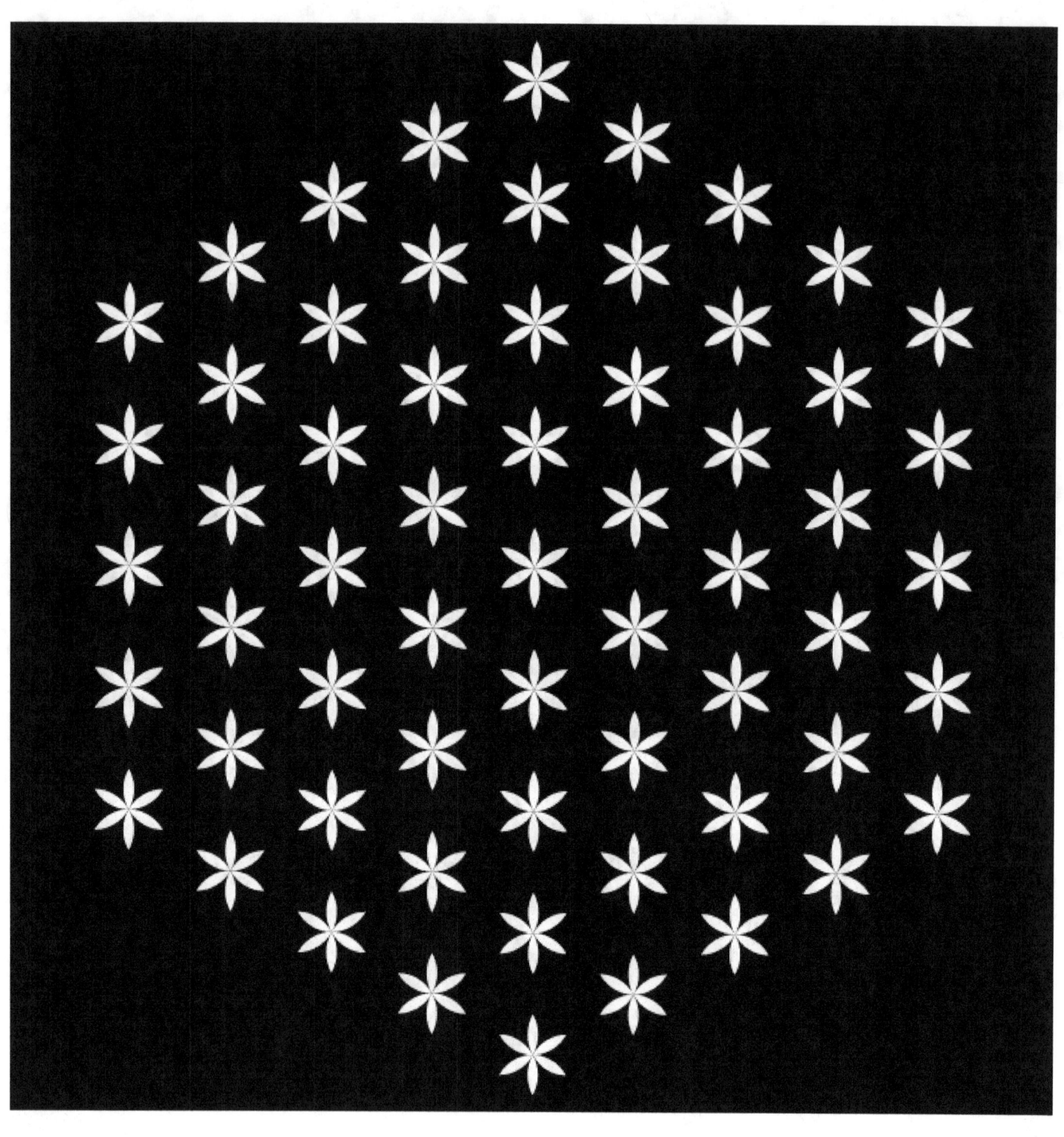

# Checkered Hexagon

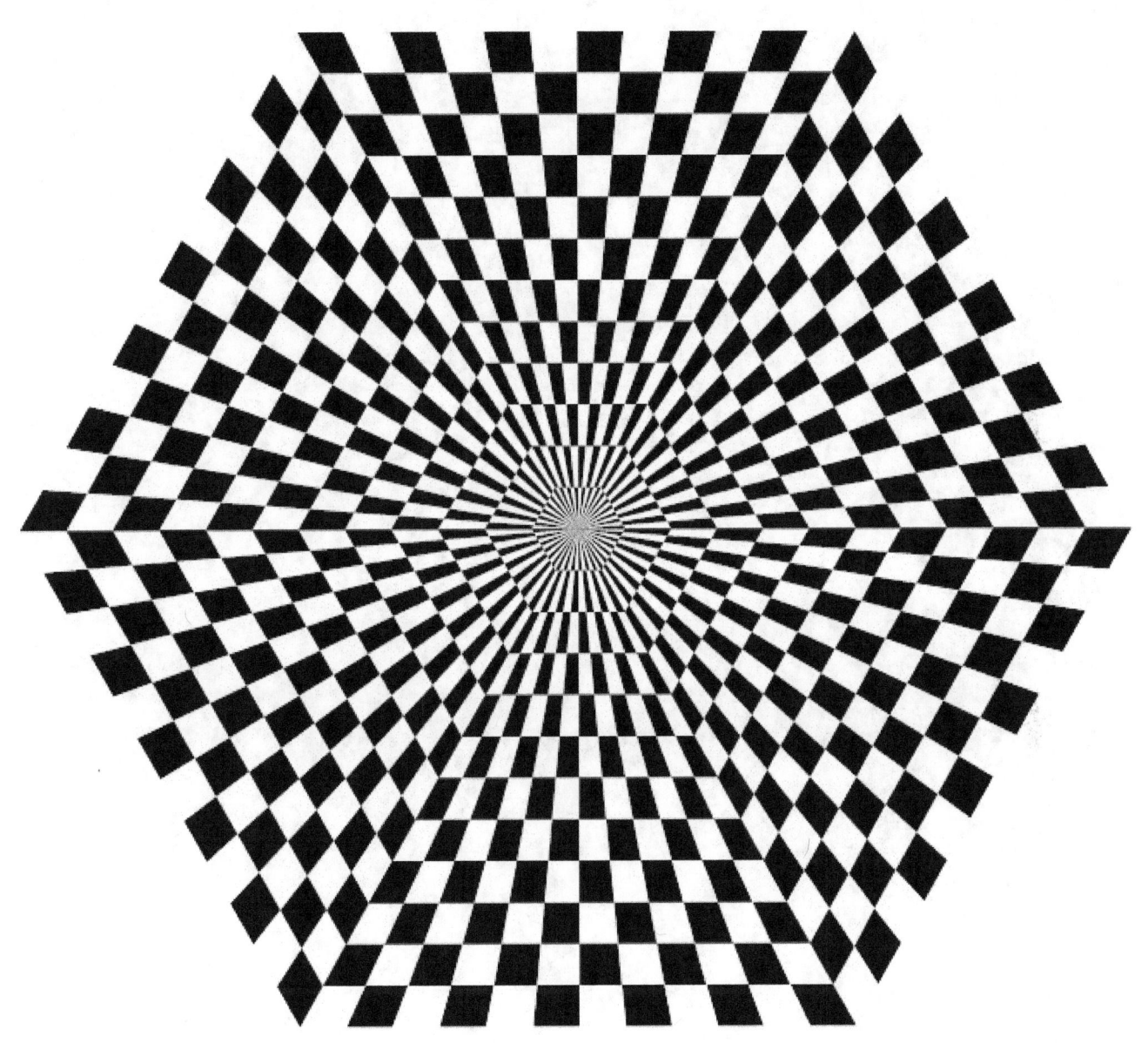

# Triquetra

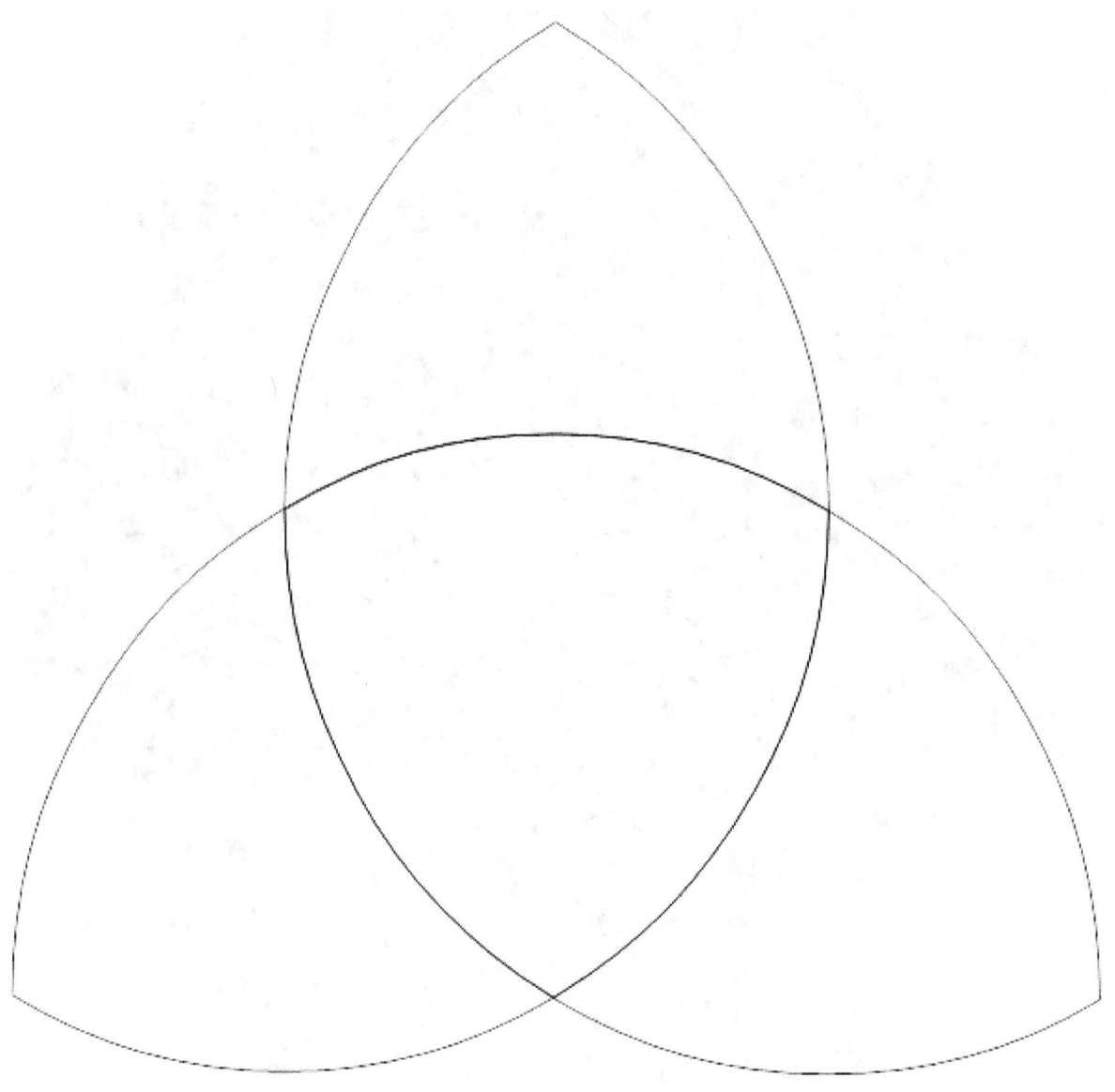

# Square Dancers Black and White

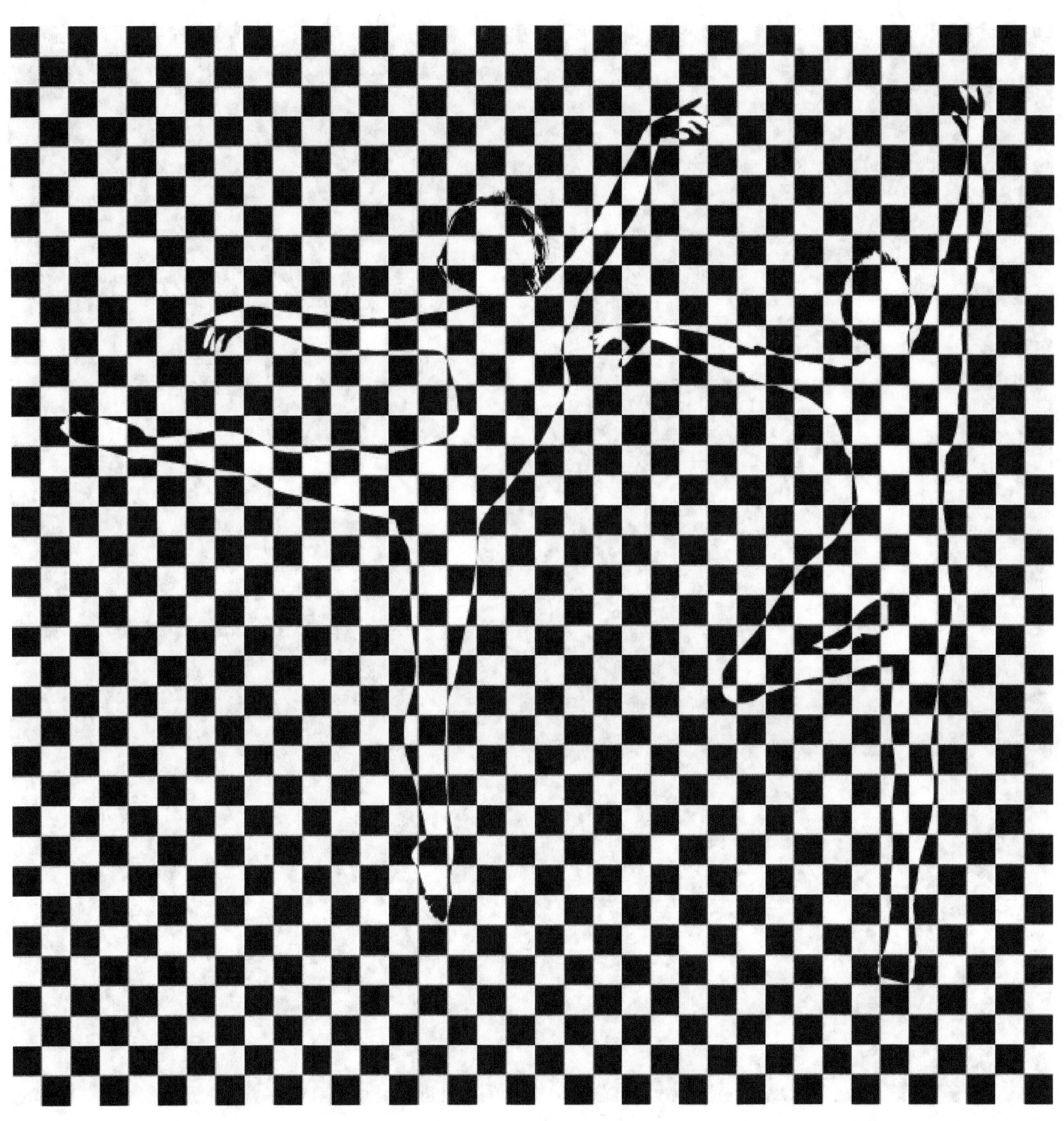

# Chessboard 36x36

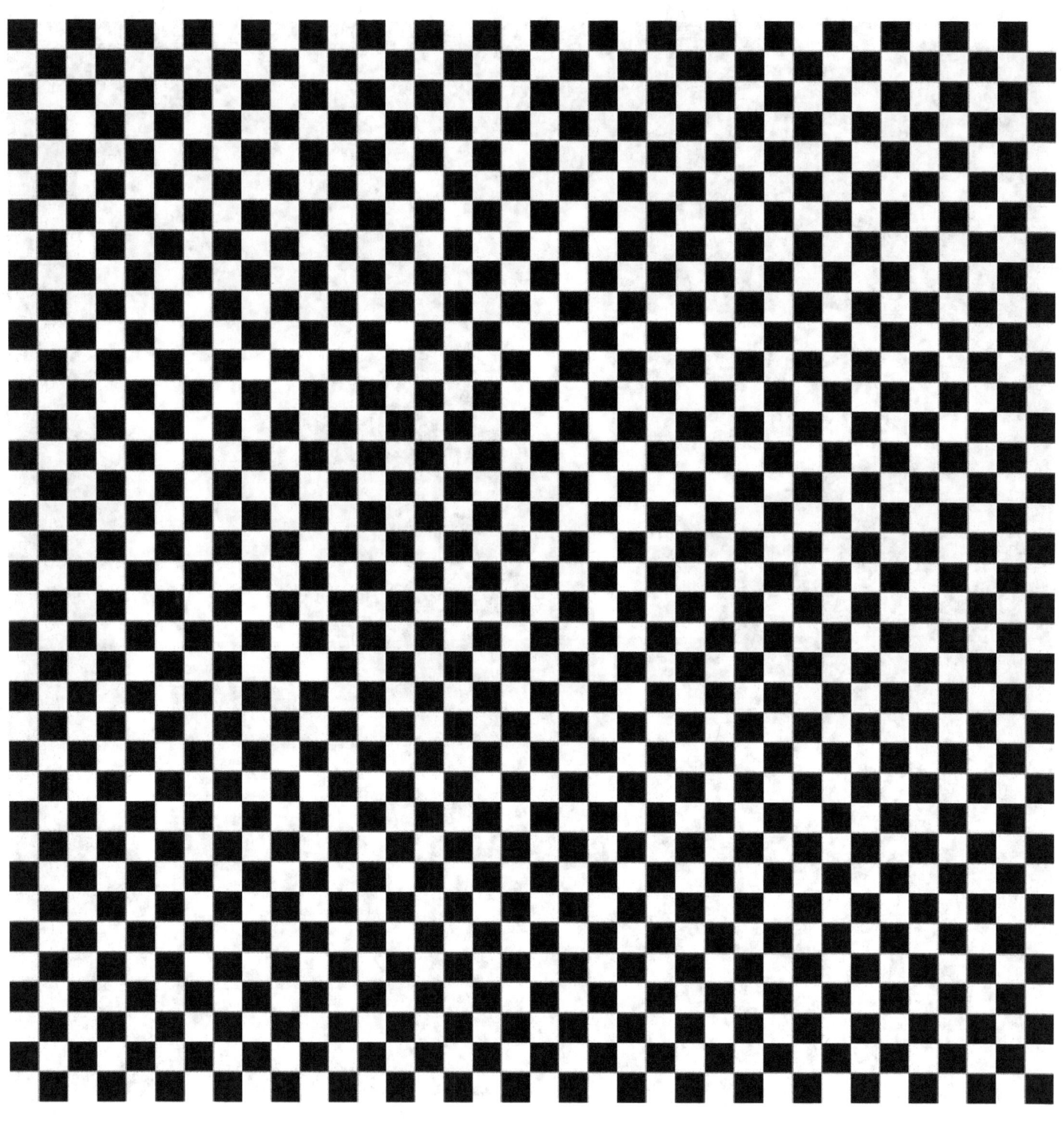

# Tunnel of Distraction

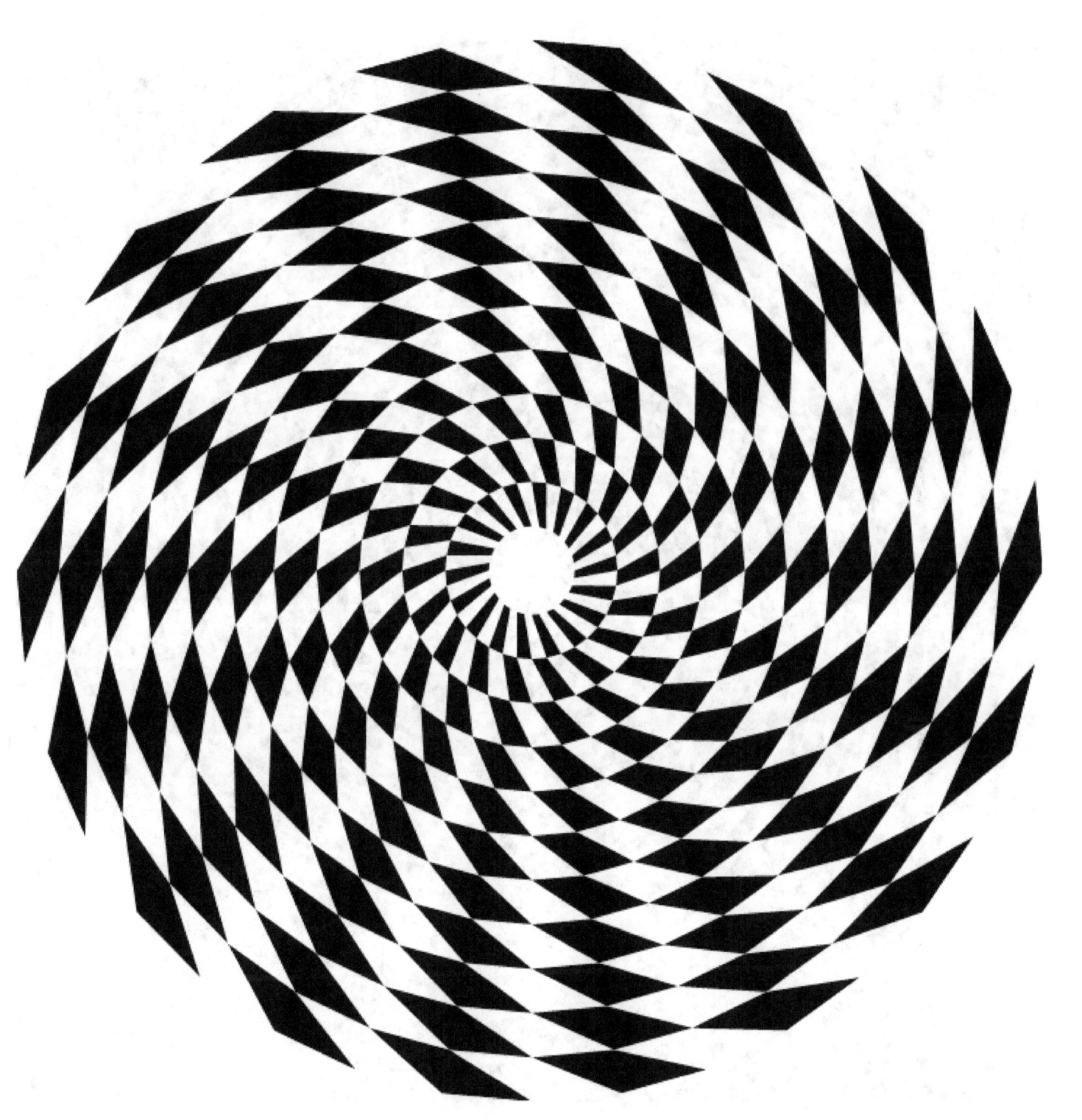

# Tunnel of Distraction Remix

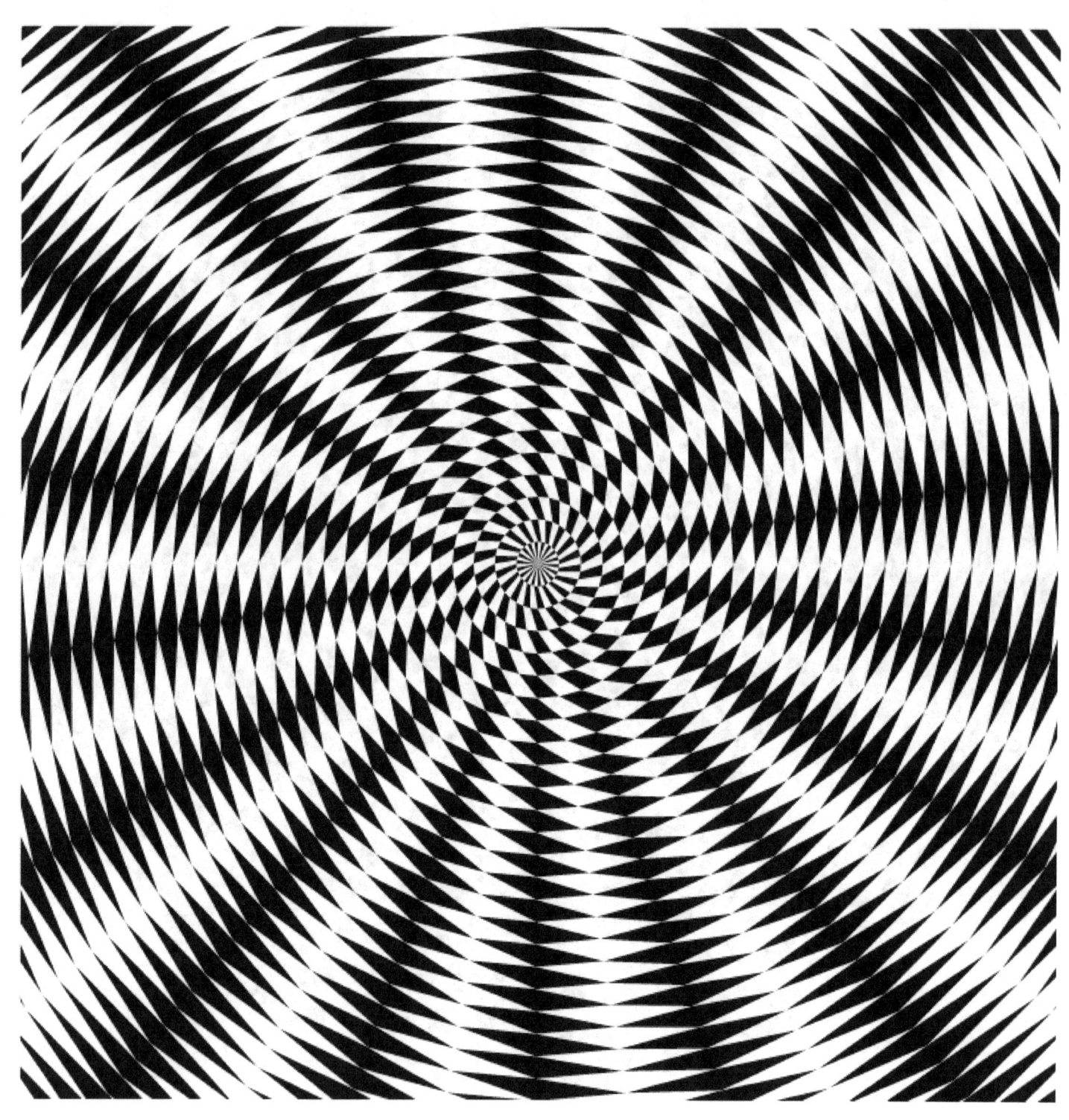

# Duck

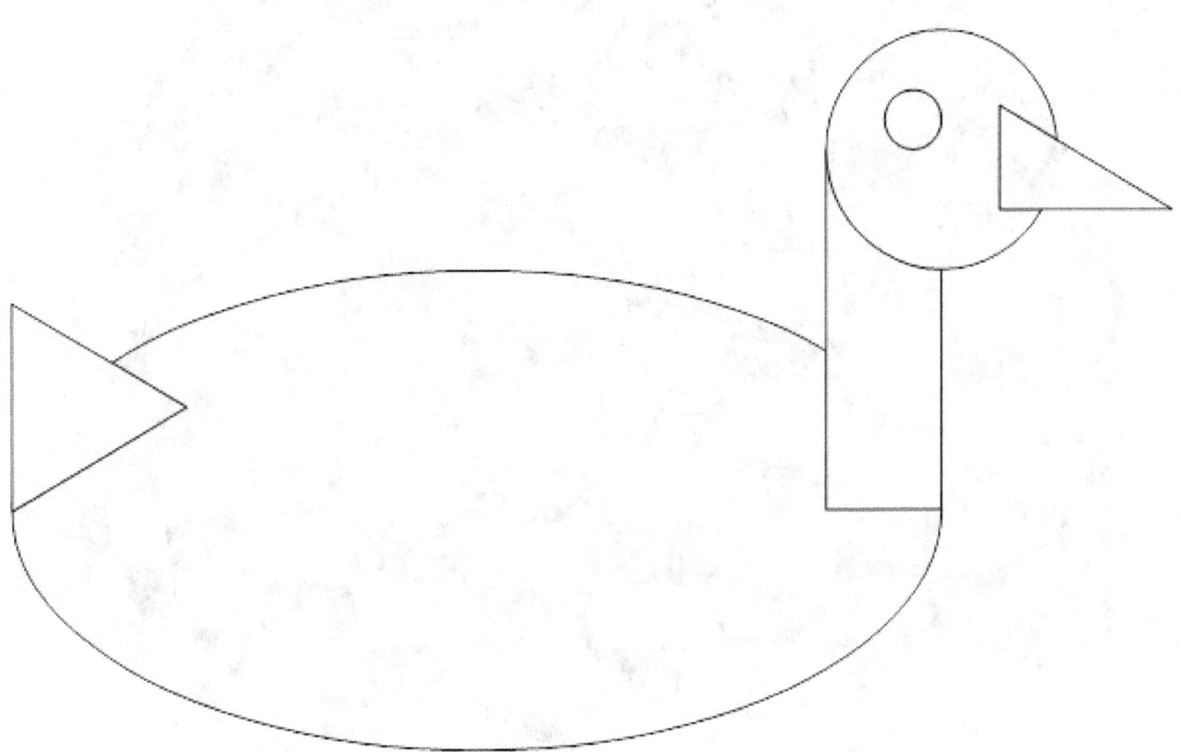

# Blender Checkersphere 2 Color

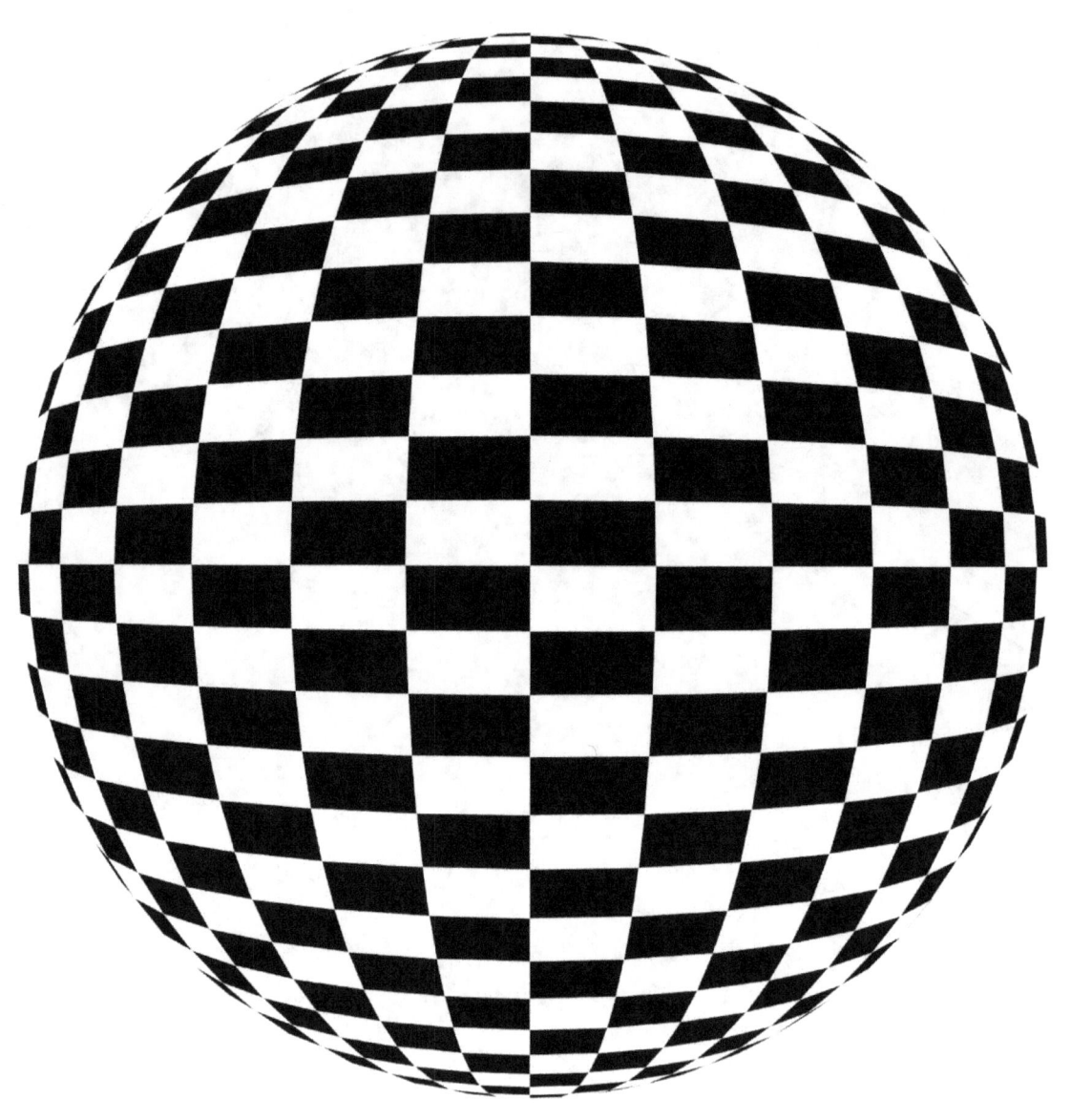

# Chessboard 18x18 rotated 45 40 pixels

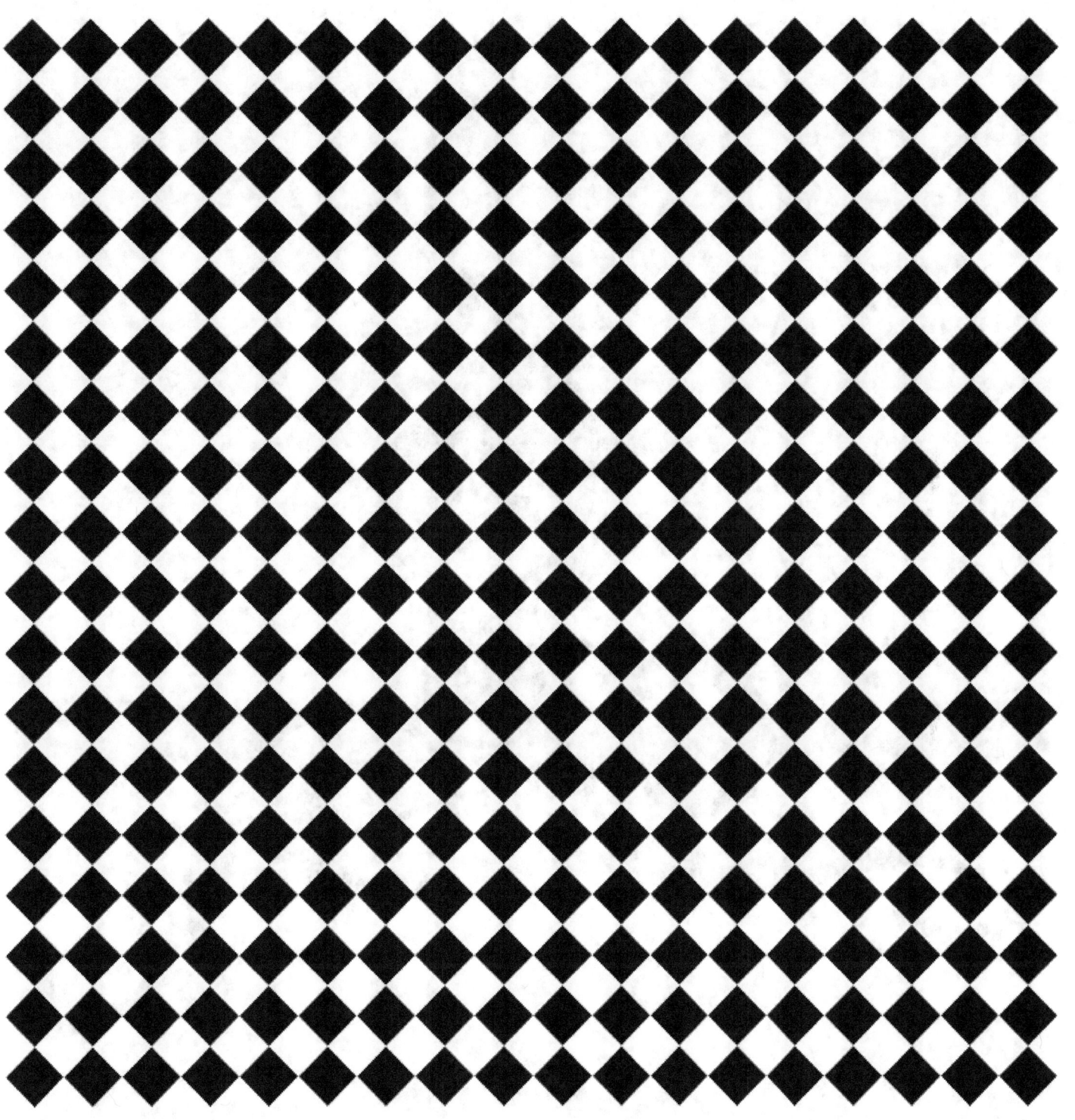

# Treble Clef Triangle

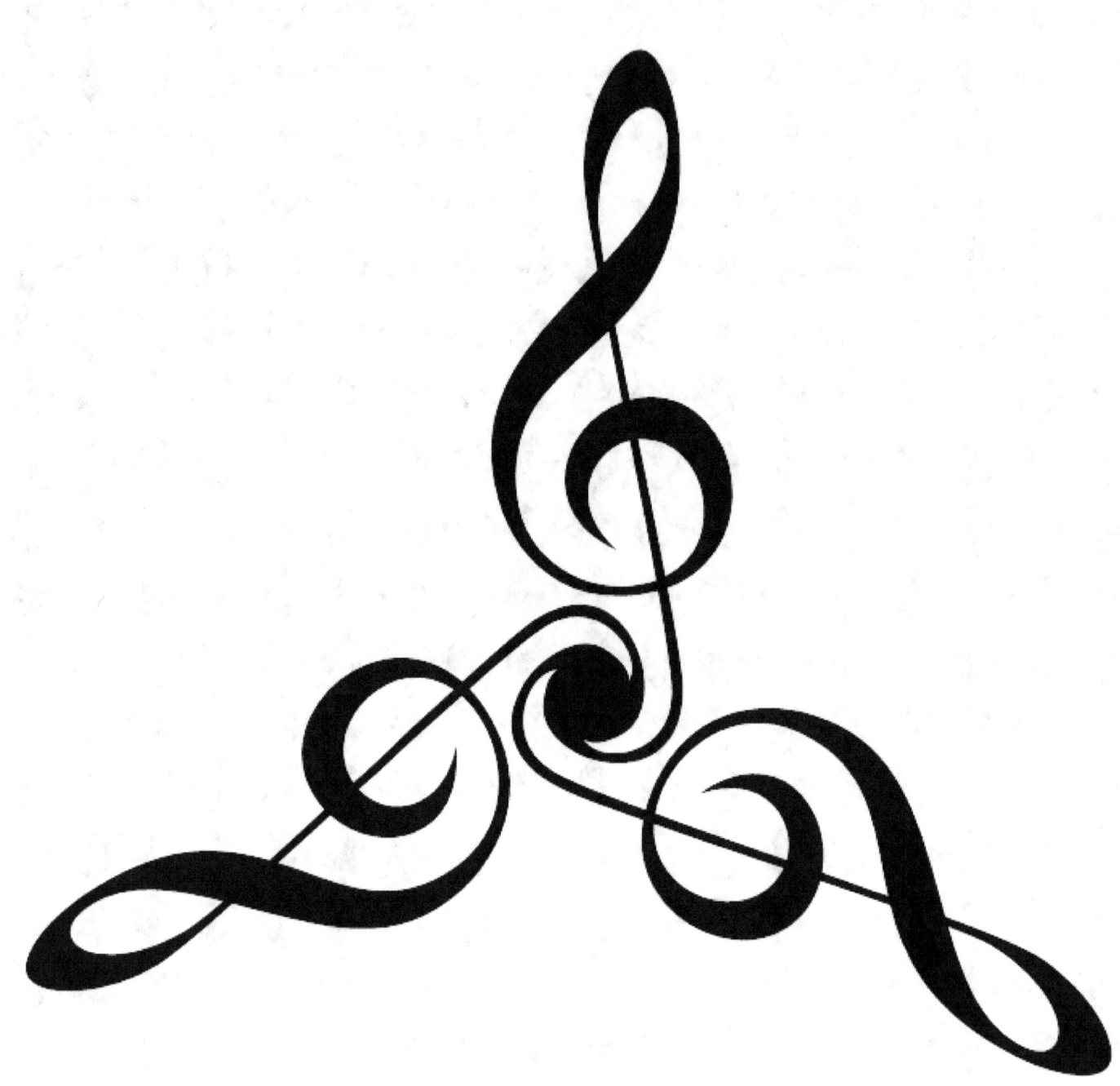

# Treble Clef Square

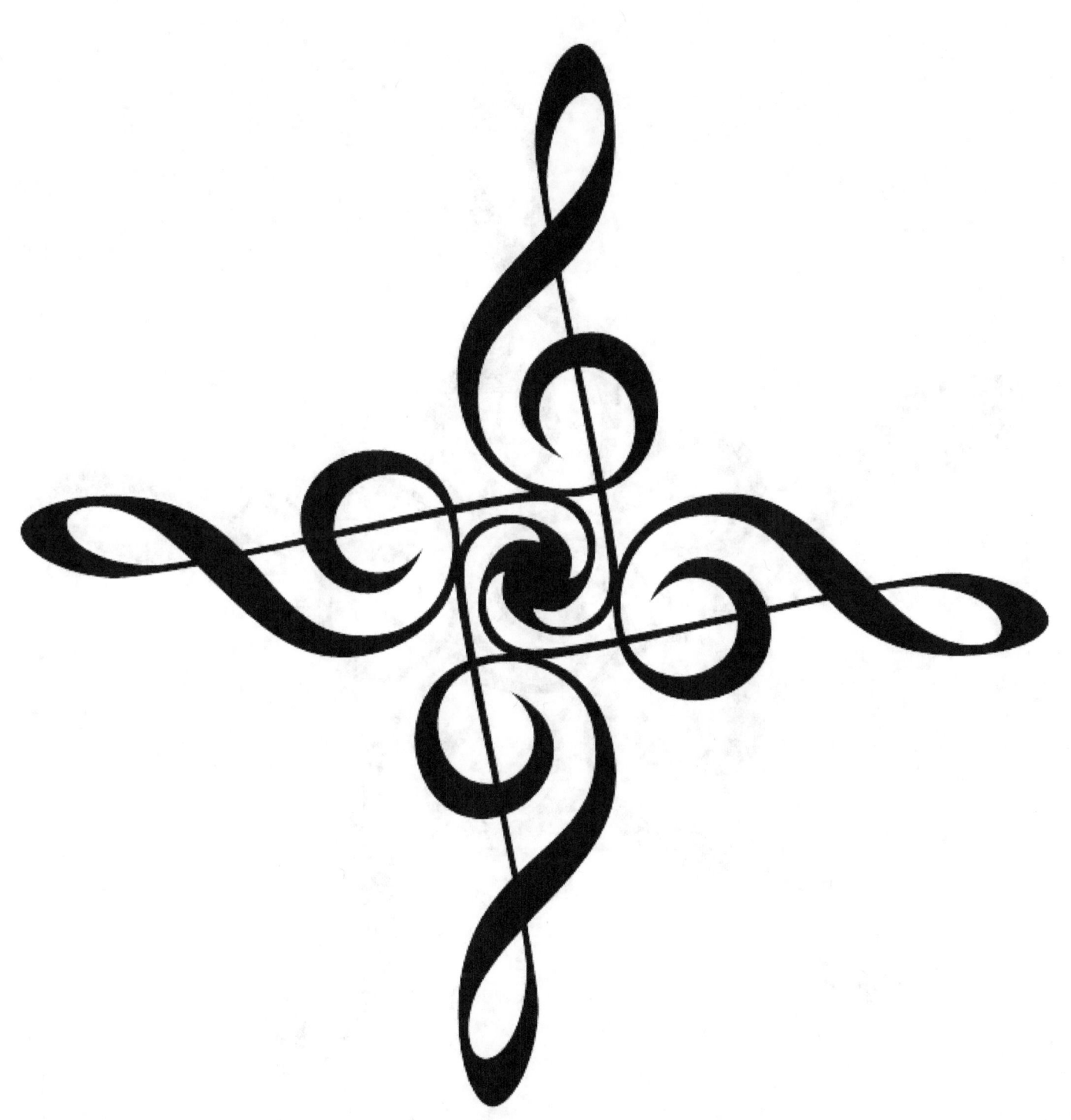

# Treble Clef Pentagon

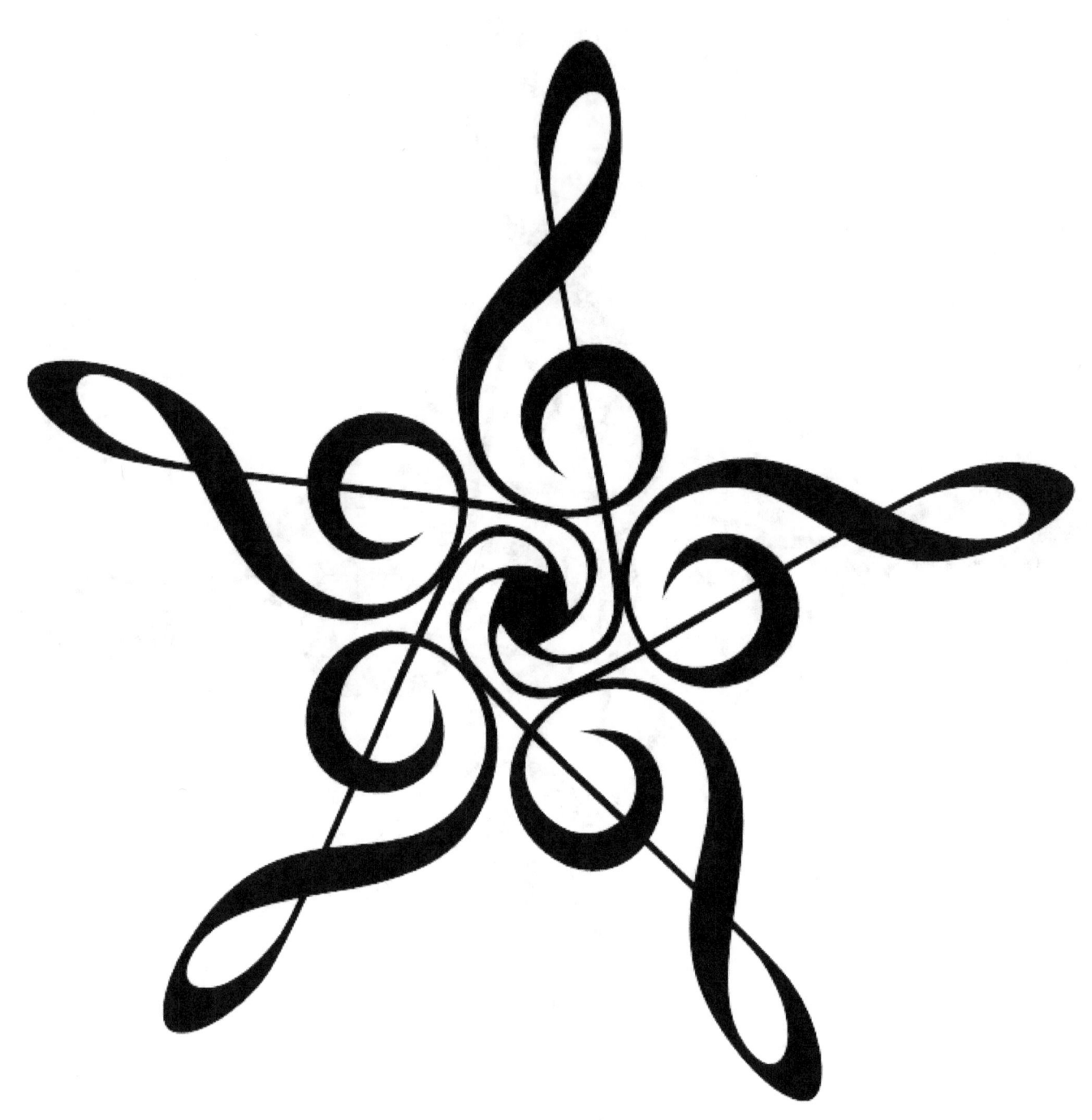

# Treble Clef Hexaflower

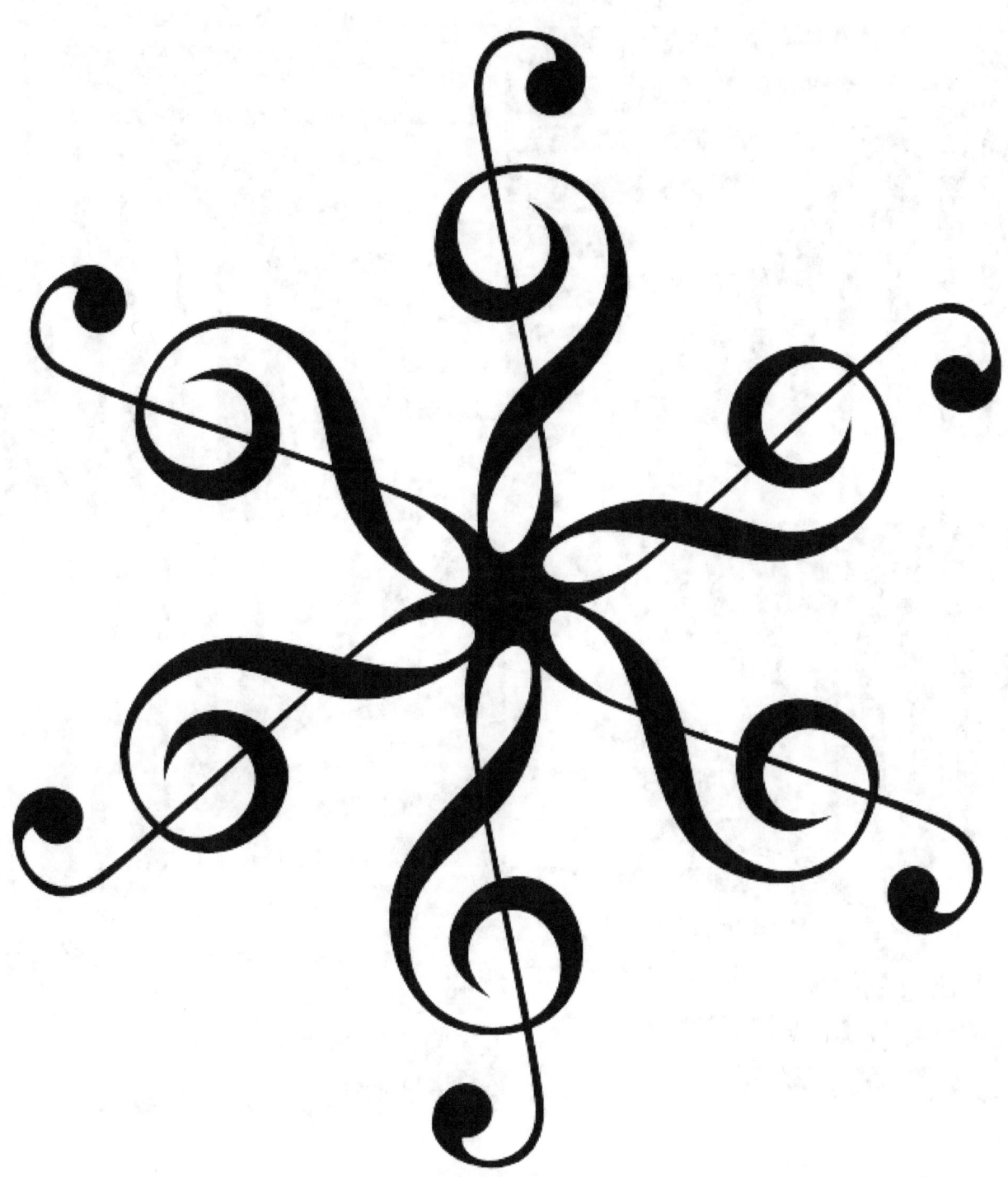

# Angular Atrocity

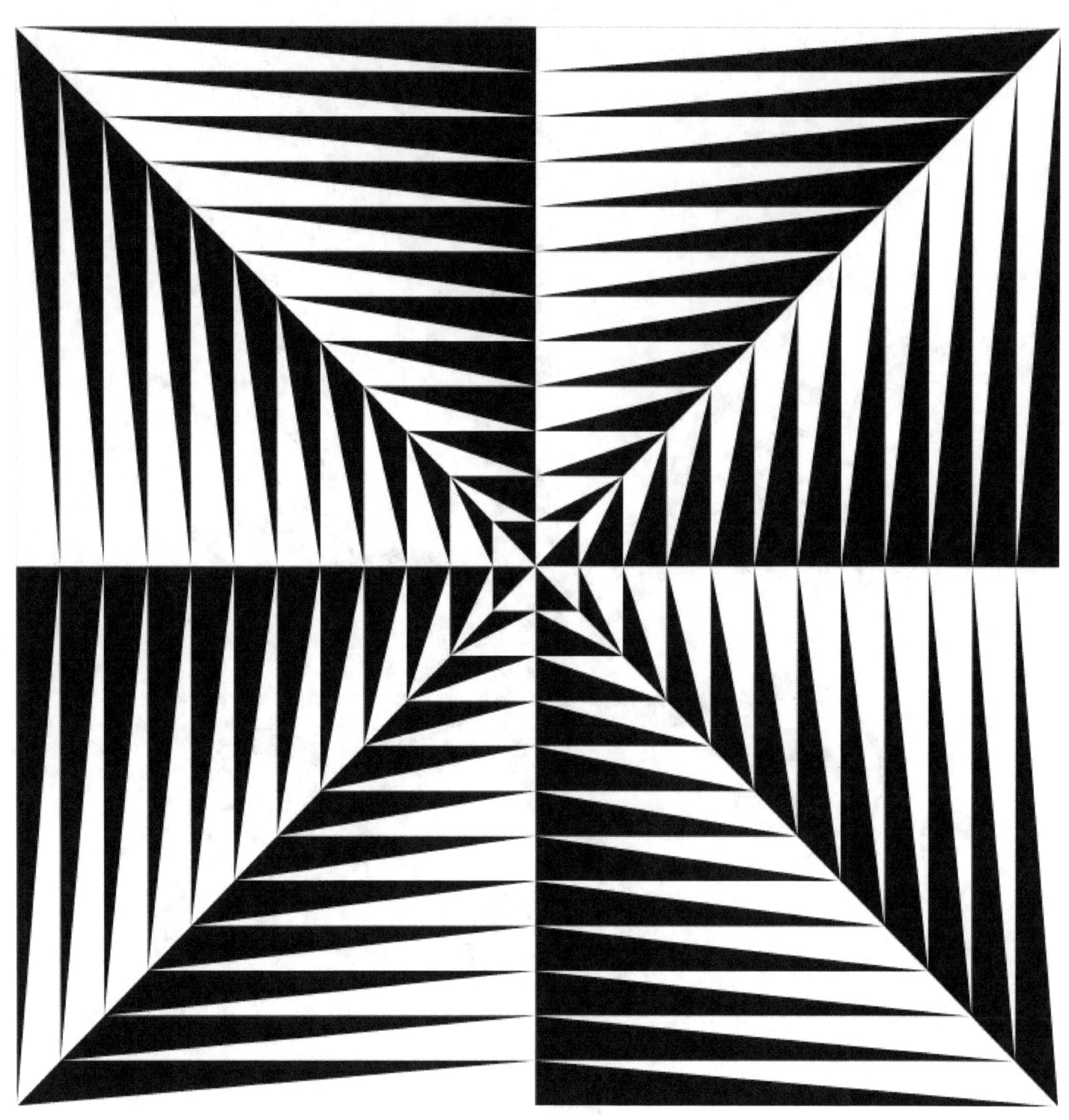

# Star Face

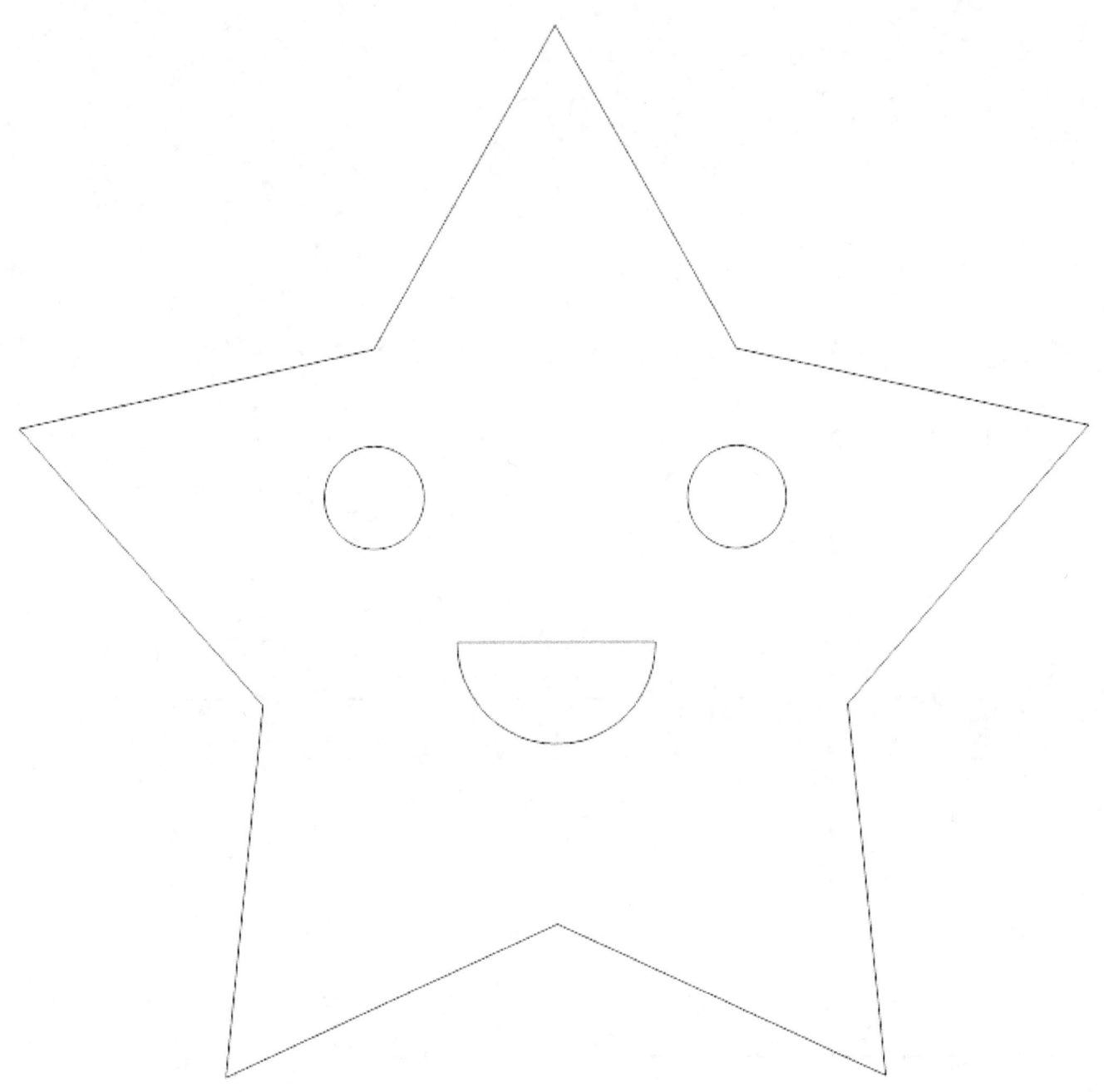

# Triangle Spiral Detail

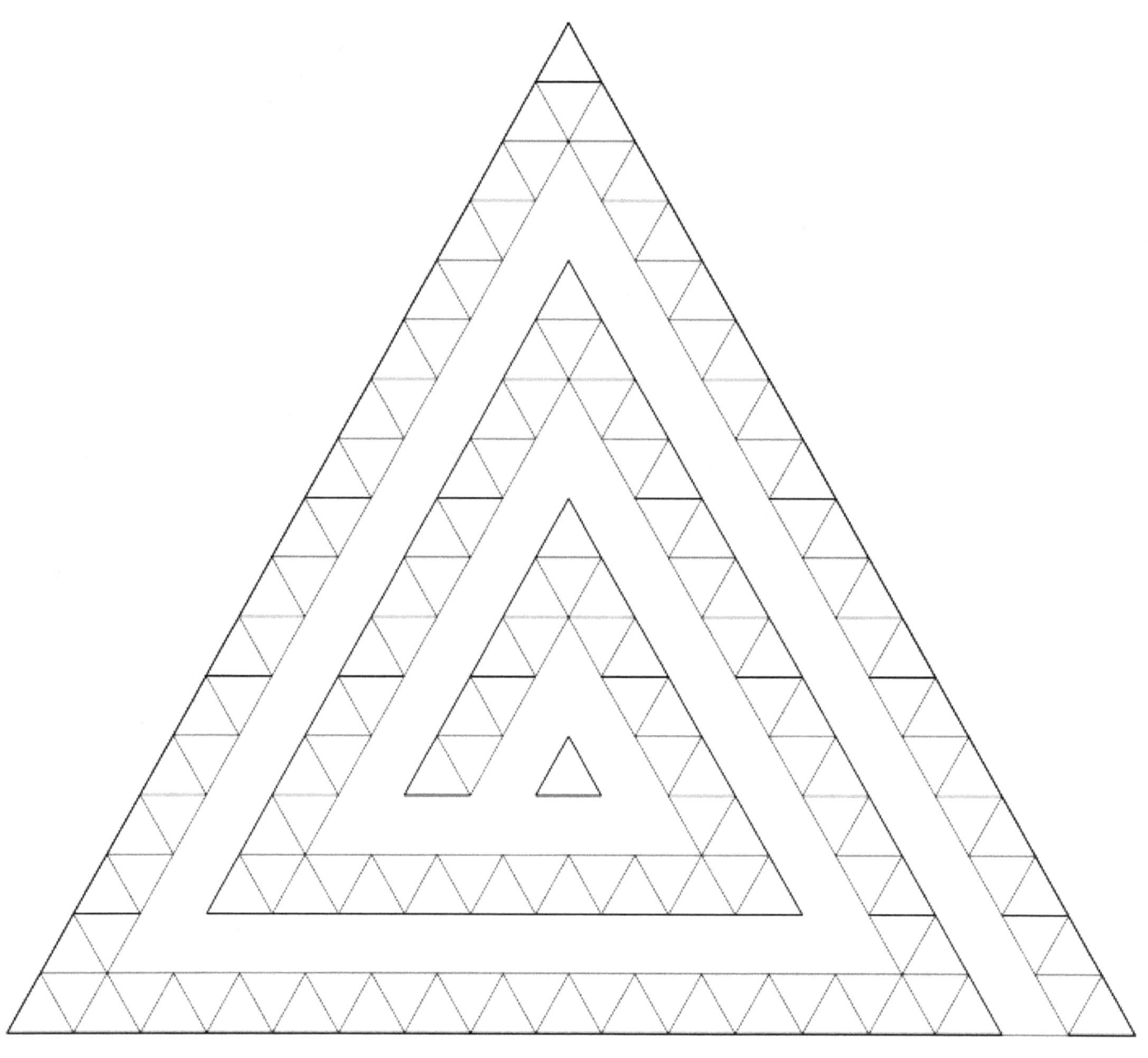

# Square Horse

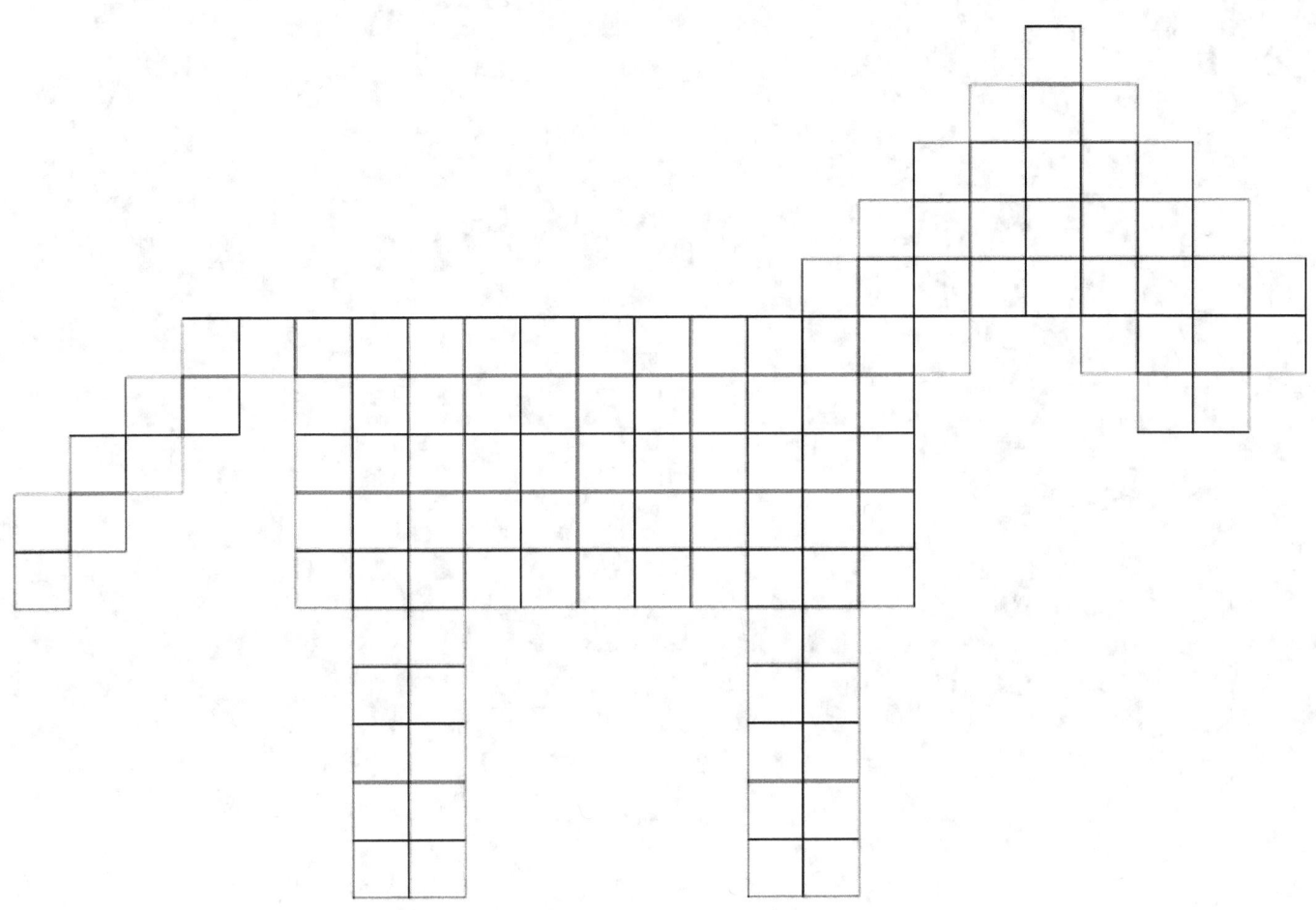

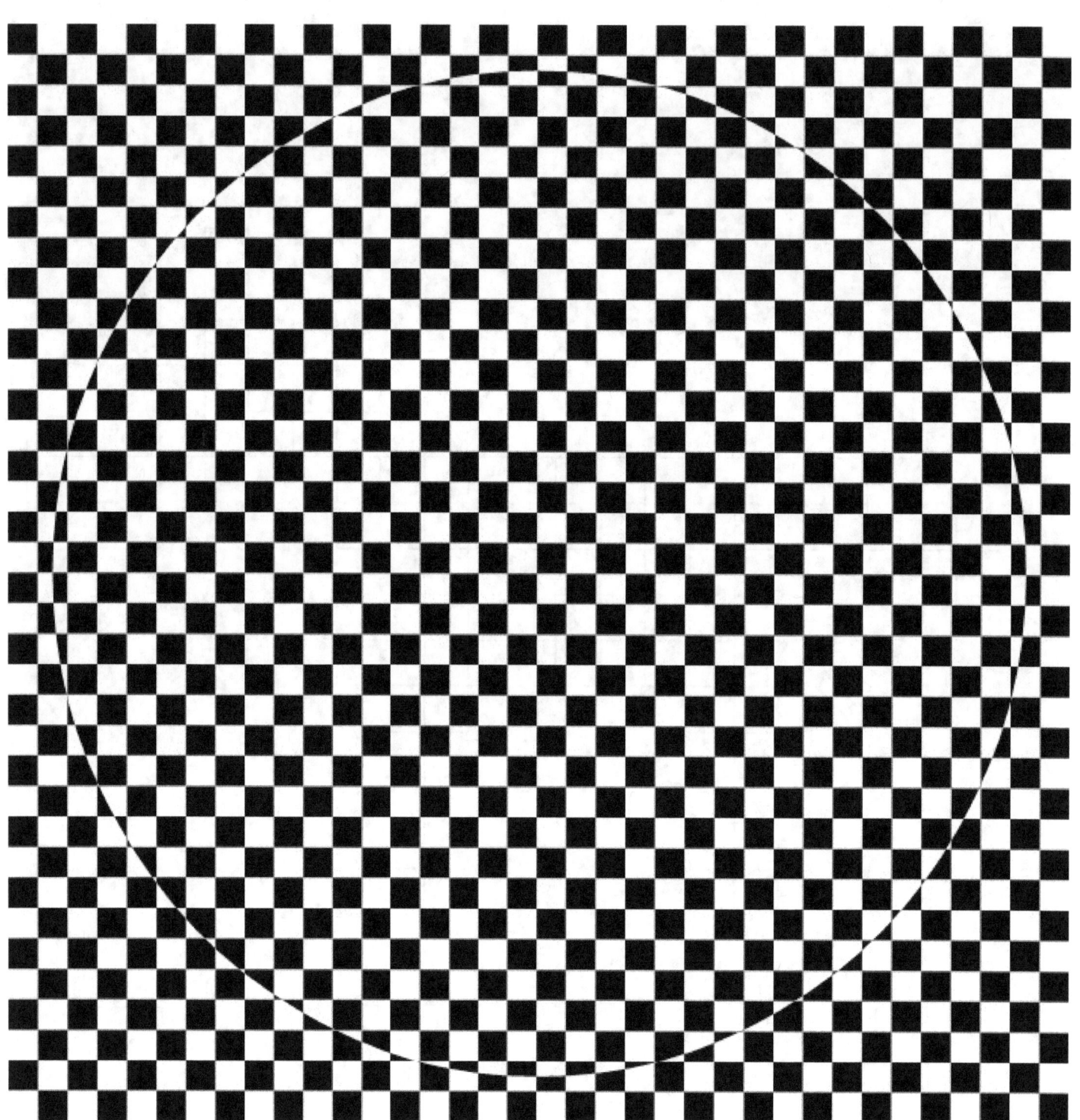

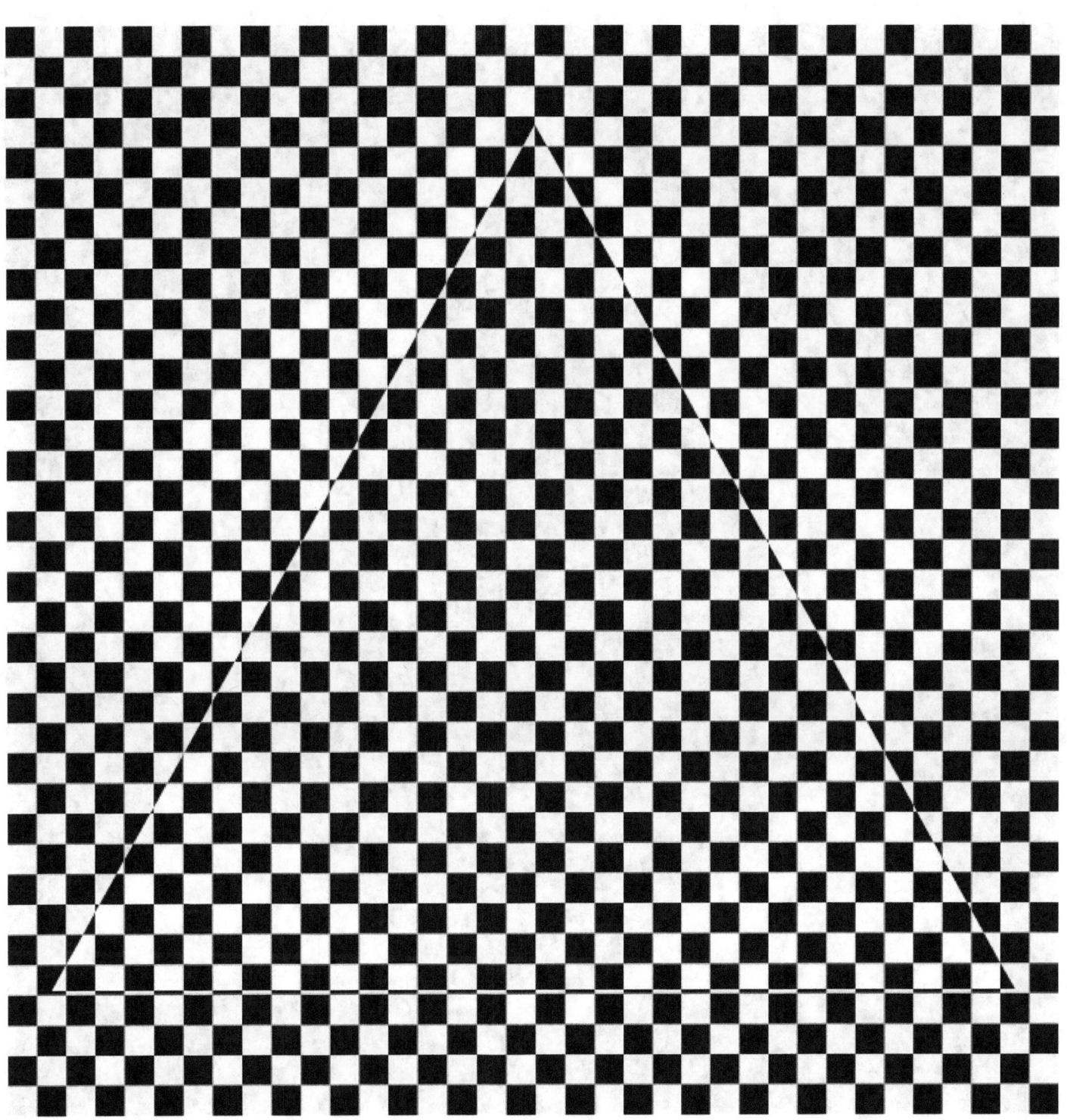

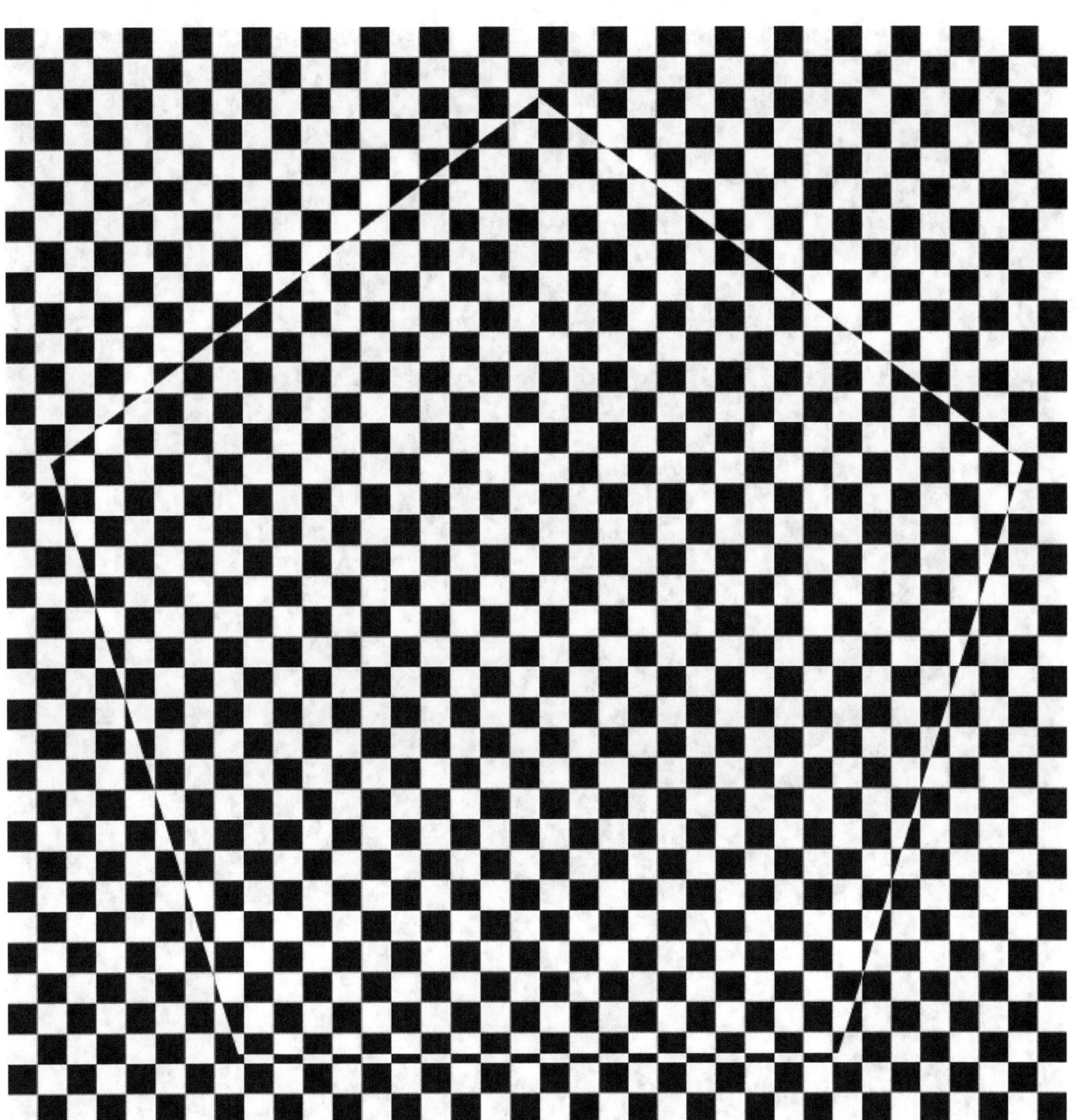

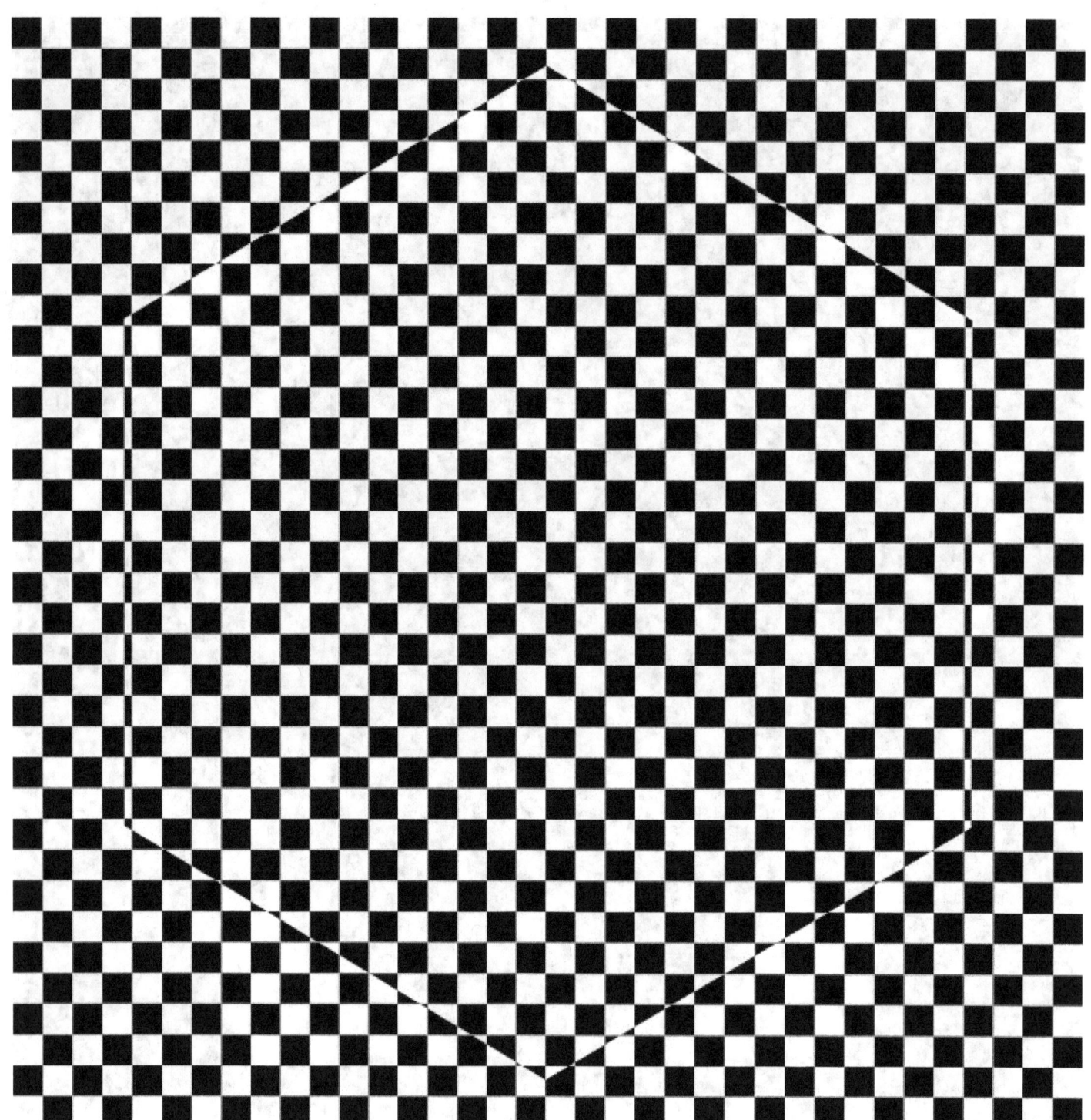

# Checkered Square Tunnel

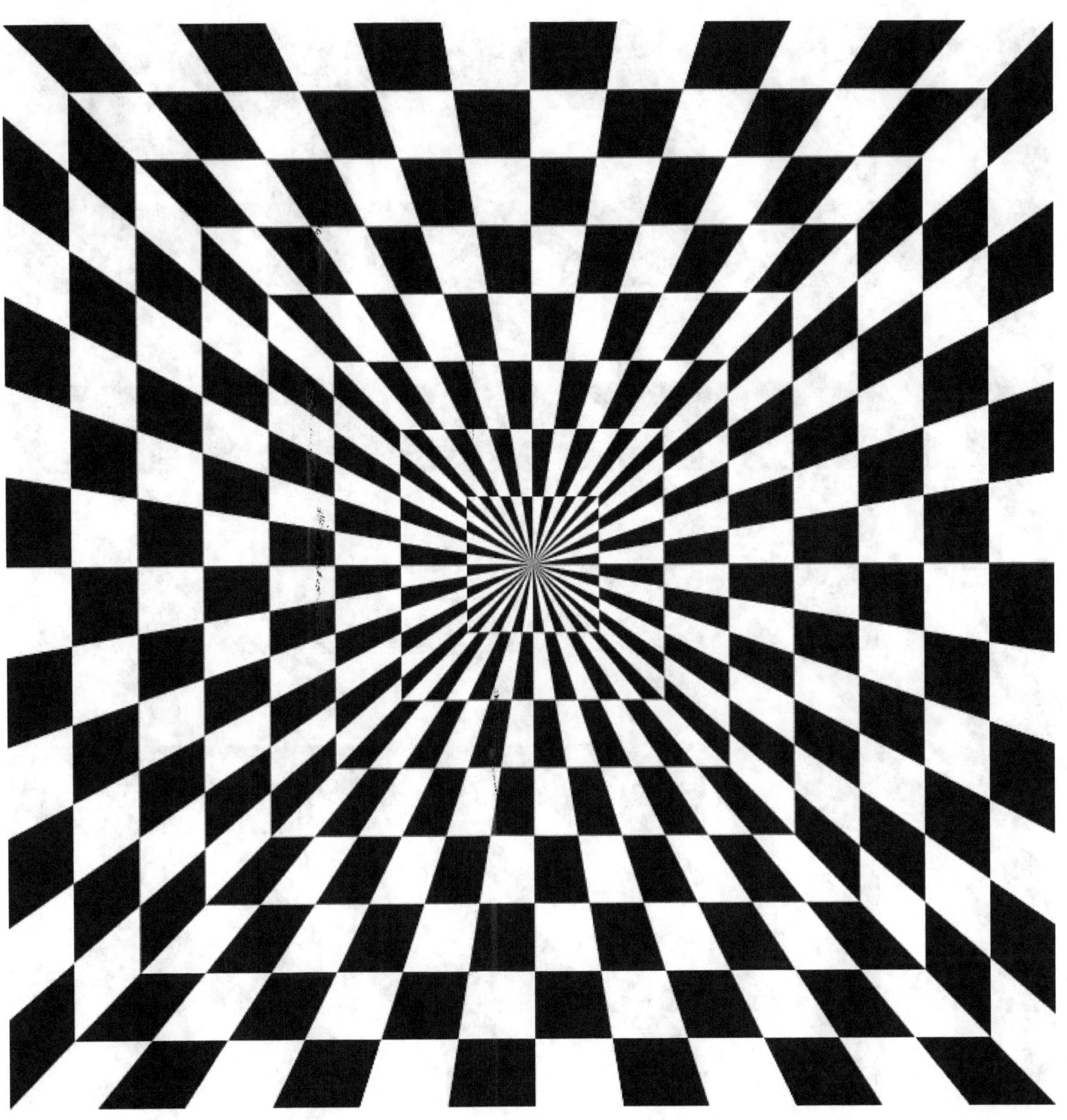

# Houndstooth 12x12

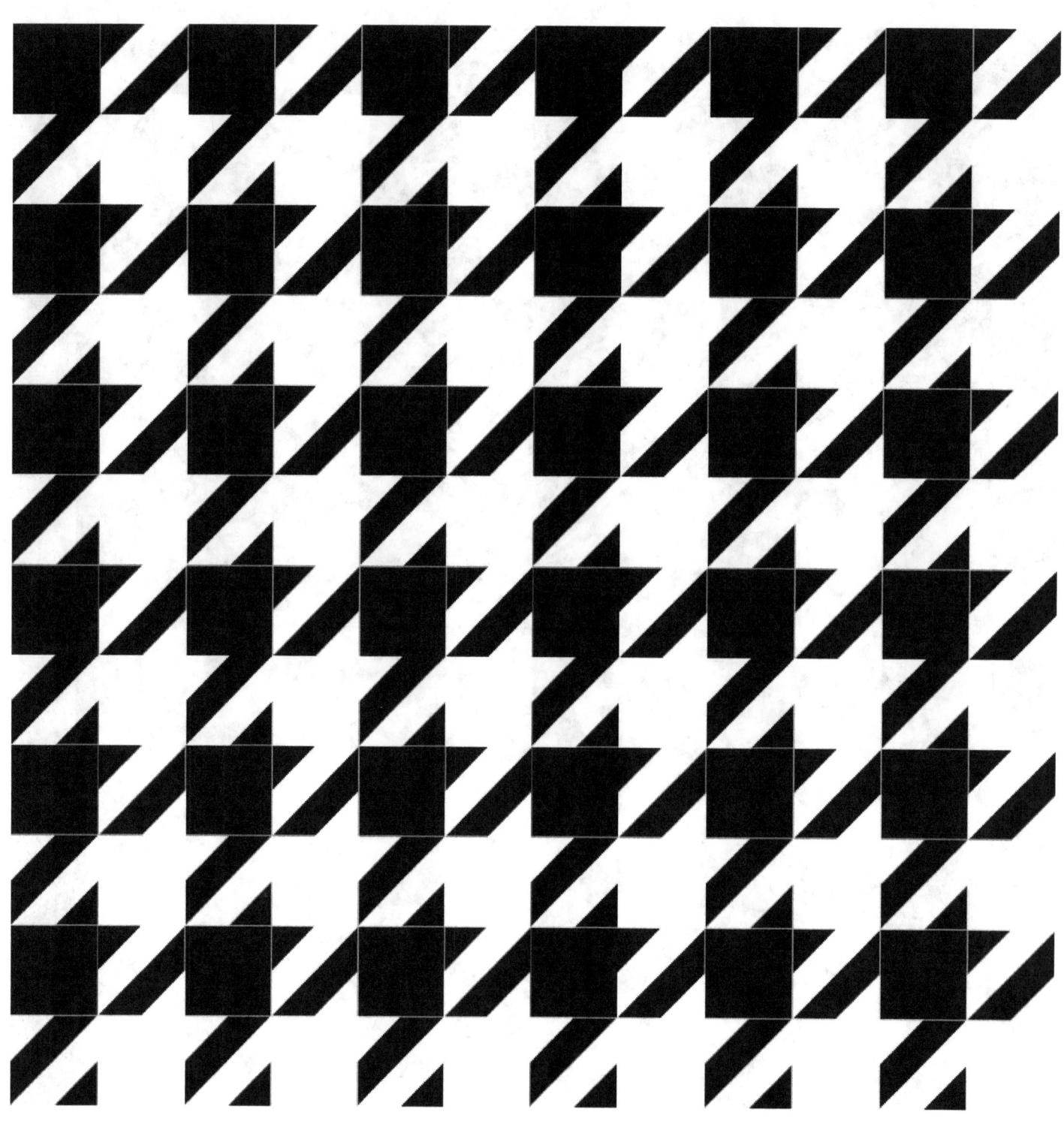

# The End

I hope you enjoyed this book full of art! Please contact me if you would like me to do some customized art for your needs. In addition to the links and email address included on the first page, you may also want to Facebook friend me for the latest stuff I tend to upload there.

https://www.facebook.com/chandlerklebs

I also revived my old art blog from 2013. There is not all that much on it now but I'm hoping to update it whenever there is big news about my art and what I'm working on.

https://chandlerklebsart.wordpress.com/

www.ingramcontent.com/pod-product-compliance
Lightning Source LLC
Chambersburg PA
CBHW062333220526
45469CB00008B/2703